THE
SOCIAL CONTRACT
WITH BUSINESS

—THE————————
SOCIAL CONTRACT
WITH BUSINESS

BEYOND THE QUEST FOR GLOBAL SUSTAINABILITY

JOPIE COETZEE

Library of Congress Control Number: 2012901214
ISBN: Hardcover   978-1-4691-5617-0
                 Softcover   978-1-4691-5616-3
                 Ebook   978-1-4691-5618-7

To order additional copies of this book, contact:
Xlibris Corporation
0-800-644-6988
www.xlibrispublishing.co.uk
Orders@xlibrispublishing.co.uk
303506

To Pieternel

for her wisdom, love, and courage

Contents

Acknowledgements

It feels as if my entire life was merely a preparation to write this book: from a boy on an African cattle farm, to an international business executive, to a scholar of business science.

Over the past sixty years, remarkable individuals shaped me in many ways. In particular:

My parents, Jooste and Marietjie, who taught me the fundamental values enshrined in this book and gave me the best education they could afford. *This book is your gift to the future!*

My wife, Pieternel, who stood by me through all the twists and turns of research and the writing of this book over the past eight years. *This book is your gift to the future!*

My family, friends, and colleagues who encouraged me to make my research available to a wider audience. *This book is your gift to the future!*

Because I have been standing on the shoulders of giants, I wish to acknowledge the wisdom from global leaders and thinkers whose names have been cited in this book. I trust that you will find joy in hearing the echoes of your voice inspiring and empowering others to continue your life's work. *This book is your gift to the future!*

The many unknown people from around the world whose voices highlighted the grotesque injustices they are facing, and their hope for a better world. And, all those decision-makers who listened and acted upon your plight. Your wisdom, love, and courage inspired me. *This book is your gift to the future!*

I am humbled by all the means of grace given to me to produce a work like this.

Soli Deo Gloria.

Author's Note to the Reader

This book introduces a breakthrough to global sustainability by synthesising Western, Eastern and Southern values, aspirations, and knowledge into one priceless diamond!

For too long the social contract with business remained shrouded in the mystique of theory development, frustrating scholars to expand the boundaries of knowledge.

For too long the social contract with business remained vague, unwritten, and suspect of undermining the profit motive of the firm, denying business leaders the richness of wisdom.

From paradigm-busting research, the Social Contract with Business was discovered within more than 100 scholarly works and more than 1,000 insights from today's global leaders from around the world. Their insights have been enriched by the wisdom, love, and courage of Nobel laureates.

In a conversational style, I am taking you on a journey away from today's world of destructive globalisation. Slowly, meticulously, and excitingly you are introduced to a new global agenda, a new mode of doing business as an organ of society; new wisdom, new success criteria, a new language, a new canon of business knowledge, and a new paradigm for business leadership education.

This conversation has been enriched with more than 100 practical examples and more than 100 reflection points. I also address typical expressions of doubt and expose more than 50 leadership blind spots and fallacies that keep you below the glass ceiling.

The book concludes with application guidelines in a strategy workshop format for business leaders on how to apply the Social Contract with Business in their organisations. For business educators a blueprint is given to develop a new generation of business leaders.

This book is about the Social Contract with Business as a means to deliver humanity's global sustainability mandate. It's written for business leaders and for all other movers and shakers who wish to conduct their affairs in a business-like and meaningful manner in any country, and any sector of human endeavour.

This book will inspire and empower you to break the glass ceiling to the kind of world you have always dreamed of . . . hoped for . . . prayed for.

May the application of the Social Contract with Business become *your gift to the future!*

Jopie Coetzee
Johannesburg, March 2012

A Guided Tour of this Book

All the paradigm-busting 'newness' in this book may be overwhelming to you. This may even lead to a cultural shock as you learn about new wisdoms from the West, East, or South.

Therefore, before we begin reading, let's take a guided tour of what lies ahead by studying the roadmap below. Thereafter, I will explain some unusual terms and concepts that I will be using as we tour through this book. I trust that this guided tour will make your reading safari exciting and life-changing as you enter the unknown world of the *Social Contract with Business*.

Golden thread	⟶			
Objective of writing	To sensitise you	To direct you	To inspire you	To empower you
Focus of writing	Antecedents	Research	Passage to . . .	Application
Core questions	What do people from the West, East, and South aspire to?	How can these aspirations be validated?	What is the link between aspirations and application?	How to deliver what humanity aspires to?
Sections of the book	Part 1 Change, yes, but to what?	Part 2 A research-based answer to the previous question	Part 3 The Social Contract with Business	Part 4 Applying the Social Contract with Business
Chapters	1,2	3,4,5	6,7,8	9,10,11,12

'A world of inclusive globalisation' (WOIG) is the world scenario driven by two powerful global forces, namely, the need to improve human security and the need to eradicate systemic poverty through responsible business models.

'**A world of destructive globalisation**' (WODG) is the world scenario that is the exact opposite of a world of inclusive globalisation, that is, reduced human security and increased poverty are irrelevant consequences of business models.

'**BRICS countries**' implies a trade block representing the developing world. The BRICS countries are Brazil, Russia, India, China, and South Africa who collectively control around 40 per cent of the global population and around 15 per cent of global wealth.

'**Business**' implies all forms of enterprises that conduct their affairs in a professional management manner such as companies, societal organisations, and government departments. In other words, it's business in its broadest sense.

'**Conscientização**' is the Portuguese root word for 'conscientisation' (i.e., a conscience-based critical awareness), which describes an educational paradigm aimed at developing subjects who can deliver a specific kind of future. In this book 'conscientisation' implies such an educational paradigm that sculpts business leaders who can deliver a WOIG.

'**Critical metasynthesis**' is a paradigm-busting research methodology that seeks new insights, new trends, and new truths within known and related knowledge. It challenges the status quo and opens new knowledge and new areas of application. It's a game-changer research method.

'**G3 countries**' implies a trade block representing the developed world. The G3 countries are the United States of America, the European Union, and Japan who collectively control around 40 per cent of the global wealth and around 15 per cent of the global population.

'**Global**' includes the regional and the local.

'**Global Icons**' are those individuals who have been selected by way of search criteria in the critical metasynthesis research methodology. Hence, they have been selected independently from my personal bias. The Global Icons are from two spheres of global influence, namely, business, societal, and political leaders from the G3 and BRICS countries who have the power and the means to act as global game-changers (collectively these countries represent around 55 per cent of global wealth and 55 per cent of global population) and the Nobel laureates of economics, peace, science, and literature over the past ten years who have been honoured for their wisdom, love, and courage as global heart and mind changers.

'**Humanity**' implies today's 7 billion people from all Western, Eastern, and Southern countries. Their collective reasonable values and aspirations are being represented by the Global Icons.

'**Human security**' implies all forms of security that a person needs to live a full and meaningful life that's free of 'threats without borders', dysfunctional societal and political behaviour, and the devastation of irresponsible business models. In other words, it's human security in its broadest sense.

'**Kairos event**' (καιρός event) is that long-awaited decisive event after which things are never the same again. In this book it is that systemic change that business leaders need to set in motion that will drive the turnaround to a WOIG.

'**Kosoryoku**' is a Japanese term that describes the nature of the oncoming future. In this book it is used as the end-purpose statement of sustainable development, that is, humanity's global sustainability mandate to its leaders.

'Poverty' implies all people who have an income of less that US$2 per day. Indications are that around 70 per cent of humanity (i.e., 4.9 billion people) falls in this category.

'Socratic dialogue' is named after the Greek philosopher Socrates who lived during 469 and 399 BC and is considered to be one of the founders of Western philosophy. His legacy lives on today as a guardian of the truth. His paradigm-busting thoughts were considered to corrupt the minds of young people. When given the choice by a court of law to either drink poison or to withdraw his thoughts, he chose death rather than to forsake the truth. In this research technique a question is asked that the questioner does not know the answer of. Once an answer is found, a new and more penetrating question is asked to uncover a new layer of insight. This kind questioning continues in an increasingly focussed manner until a core truth is found.

'Threats without borders' is a term used to describe a collection of globalised threats impacting on local communities, who are powerless to defend themselves against the impact thereof because the traditional notions of national security and national sovereignty have become obsolete, namely, poverty, infectious disease, global warming and environmental degradation, armed conflict, organised crime, terrorism, and weapons of mass destruction. This term was first used by an Egyptian leader, Mohammed ElBaradei (Nobel Laureate for Peace—2005, for his work as Chairman of the International Atomic Energy Agency).

In those chapters dealing with the validation of my research (i.e., Chapter 5: A Brutal Reality Check) and the passage to the application thereof (i.e., Chapter 8: Case Studies from Around the World), powerful wisdoms from Global Icons are quoted to assist with the transition from science to application. These quotes act as midwives to birth a new way of doing business, as well as to demonstrate the practical viability thereof. You could view the Global Icons as co-writers of these chapters.

Each chapter is written in a style that best suited to achieve the objective of that chapter. Whilst reading the text you may recognise the echoes of your own and other's voices, but in a different context, namely, the context of the Social Contract with Business.

I advise the reader to read slowly and reflectively, because everything in this book is like a priceless diamond; only to be discovered if you care to search the most obvious of places, namely . . .

Well, let's now begin with Chapter 1: Listening to Voices from Around the World in order to find that priceless diamond!

PART 1

CHANGE, YES, BUT TO WHAT?

What Makes Humanity Humane?

'What I¹ mean by this [the moral minimum guiding human behaviour] can be demonstrated relatively simply by means of the Golden Rule of Humanity which we find in all the great religious and ethical traditions. Here are some of its formulations:

Confucius *(c.551-489 BCE): 'What you yourself do not want, do not do to another person' (Analects 15.23).*

Rabbi Hillel *(60 BCE-10 CE): 'Do not do to others what you would not want them to do to you' (Shabbat 31a).*

Jesus of Nazareth*: 'Whatever you want people to do to you, do also to them' (Matt. 7: 12; Luke 6: 31).*

Islam: *'None of you is a believer as long as he does not wish his brother what he wishes himself' (Forty Hadith of an-Nawawi, 13).*

Buddhism: *'A state which is not pleasant or enjoyable for me will also not be so for him; and how can I impose on another a state which is not pleasant or enjoyable for me?' (Samyutta Nikaya V, 353, 35-342, 2).*

Hinduism: *'One should not behave towards others in a way which is unpleasant for oneself: That is the essence of morality' (Mahabharata XIII, 114, 8).'*

CHAPTER 1

LISTENING TO VOICES FROM AROUND THE WORLD

In today's world of information overload, it's difficult to listen.

It is even more difficult to comprehend a trend of voices from around the world. To hear and reflect upon the actual message from these voices amidst a cacophony of noise is nearly impossible—we are simply too busy being busy.

Taking our moral compass as the Golden Rule of Humanity, let's begin to listen to voices from history, to soundless voices, to audible voices from today's leaders and thinkers, and lastly to voices from the arts.

Voices from history

In 1690, the philosopher John Locke[2] listened to voices from society and crafted his *Two Treatises of Government*, where he put two very significant concepts together into one philosophy—the theory of the radical individual and the theory of the negative state. He acknowledged the individual's right to acquire and dispose of property, the right to live his or her life as he or she sees fit, and the right to liberty of conscience and opinion. He also acknowledged that, for the sake of societal order, a government needs to be elected as the trustee of the individual's rights. Given governments' propensity to abuse power, elections need to be held regularly, with political parties tendering to act as trustee of societal values for another three to five years. With this theory, Locke laid the foundation for today's liberal democracy. Today democracy is being embraced by people from 136 countries, representing around 70 per cent of humanity.[3]

The origin of the French Revolution in 1789 may be found some 100 years earlier when John Locke acted upon the voices of ordinary people—voices yearning for liberty, equality, and fraternity. Today, these values are acknowledged as the beginning of the Age of Enlightenment, where reason is advocated as the primary source and legitimacy for authority. This is at the core of today's global society.

In 1834, slavery was abolished in the British Empire as a result of politician William Wilberforce's unrelenting pursuit of fairness, freedom, and justice. He listened to and acted upon the voices of those who had no voice in society—the slaves. Today, slavery, as old as humanity, has been abolished in all countries.

In 1989, the Berlin Wall came down. This signalled the end of a failed ideological experiment with communism. History has yet to disclose how many ordinary people died from the grave consequences of this folly, but ultimately their voices have been heard by responsible leaders. Today, millions of people from formerly closed economies are thriving under democracy and the free market.

I have taken only four examples from history to illustrate the power of listening to, and acting upon the voices of ordinary people. It's truly inspirational to learn that great and lasting leadership acts are anchored in acting upon reasonable voices calling out to live a life of meaning in the light.

Soundless voices

Can you imagine a spring without any bird-song—and no frogs—and no beetles—and no animals—and no clean fountains—and no blue sky?

This was the reality for Rachel Carson[4] when she published *Silent Spring* in 1962 on America's irresponsible use of insecticides and other pesticides. This book is credited with setting today's quest for global sustainability in motion.

Sadly, not all listened to Carson.

Today we cannot imagine the anguish of some 75-100 million people dying from bubonic fever in the late 1300s when the Black Death wiped out between 30 per cent and 60 per cent of Europe's population.[5] Similarly, today we do not hear the anguish of bees dying from another plague, humanity's insatiable consumerism fuelled by irresponsible business models, irresponsible application of insecticides, and irresponsible destruction of natural ecosystems. Honey bees pollinate around 70 per cent of all food consumed by humanity, and while scientific data is inconclusive, there are early warning signals that the world's honey bee population is collapsing, and consequently global human food security is being put at risk.[6]

Will you dare to care listening to the bees?

Now, let's listen to the footsteps of millions of desperate people, all in flight from oppressive regimes, poverty, or ecological degradation—respectively known as political refugees, economic refugees, and environmental refugees. The impact of this silent human migration into stable societies is not yet fully understood, while resulting in a silent but uneasy tolerance, and increasingly sporadic outbreaks of violence.

Here I think of the unprecedented influx of people into Europe from the Middle East and Africa. Increasingly, voices are raised about Europe losing its culture, and eventually probably also its sovereignty.[7]

I also think of India, quietly fencing off Bangladesh with a 5000-kilometre and 2-metre-high, barbed wire, and fully electrified fence with military patrols. The objective is to protect its own citizens from having its living space invaded by their poor neighbours.[8]

I also think of my own country, South Africa, which is being invaded between 4 and 11 million illegal immigrants from the rest of Africa.[9] This is an intolerable additional 10 per cent to 25 per cent burden on our social services, such as hospital services, municipal services, and the local job market. No wonder South Africa's unemployment rate is around 35 per cent, even though job creation is a government priority! Instead of protecting its own citizens' sovereign living and working space, our government is accusing society of xenophobia and forcing them into accepting this grotesque injustice—a case of shredding the social contract due to misplaced loyalty to political friends in the rest of Africa.

Let's conclude by listening to the soundless voices from the global commons.

But what is this global commons[10]?

In many parts of the world, rural people share a common piece of land outside town where you could graze your cow, collect medicinal herbs, hunt for food, socialise, or simply relax. All people have a collective responsibility to keep this common area in good stead as all depend on it as an extension of their life and well-being. This area is simply called the commons.

Now, this local concept of 'the commons' has been extended to a global scale and called the Commons Sphere. This stands together with the other spheres of organised life, namely, the Private Sphere (i.e., private ownership and the distribution of goods and services through the free market), and the Public Sphere (i.e., where governments provide goods and services to its citizens, such as schools, hospitals, and roads).

James Quilligan defines the global commons as follows:

' . . . is neither public nor private, yet underlies both. It has autonomous life because it exists at the intersection of society and nature; is grounded in our cooperation and will to survive; predates our modern rules of private property; transcends our present political boundaries, yet strengthens the duty of the nation-state to protect its citizens; reflects the interdependence of all issues and all groups; arises from the prior unity of humanity; belongs to no one, and thus to everyone; is intergenerational (from our ancestors to us, to our children, and future generations); is rooted in human and cultural potentials; expresses diversity, hope, and trust; invites participation and dialogue; empowers people with a specific framework of action; redefines the balance between freedom and responsibility; reflects shared ownership, management, and distribution of resources; promotes both efficiency and sustainability in a global open society; thrives on transparent communication and networking; is inherently spiritual, ontological, and simultaneous in world time; reveals our sovereignty as world citizens.'

The global commons is structured into three distinct categories[11], namely:

> ➤ Noosphere: Airwaves, art, connectedness, indigenous cultures, information, Internet, knowledge, languages and traditions, music, religion, sacredness, security, silence, societal values, traditions, and wisdom.
> ➤ Biosphere: Agriculture, ecosystems, fisheries, forests, gene pool of all creatures, genetic life, land, mountains, pasture, rivers, seeds, and wetlands.
> ➤ Physiosphere: Atmosphere, climate, inorganic energy, minerals, stratosphere, and the elements.

Reflecting upon the global commons and its issues, what soundless voices do you hear . . . of joy, meaning, and hope? . . . Of anger, despair, and hopelessness? . . . Of the cacophony from the arrogant and the fool?

Now, let's reflect deeply on the meaning and the implications of a voice from an ancient prophecy[12]:

When all the trees have been cut down
When all the animals have been hunted
When all the waters are polluted
When all the air is unsafe to breathe
Only then will you discover that you cannot eat money

Can there be a greater act of leadership listening to, and acting upon this voice?

Can there be a greater act of leadership cowardice ignoring this voice?

Audible voices

Let's begin to listen to the voices from today's global civil society, made audible through communication technology and social network platforms.

In this regard, I am reminded of the violent protests over high food prices during 2008. Within a matter of days, we were all stunned to see on television how desperate and hungry people resorted to violent protests against the impact of high oil prices on their daily supply of basic foods. In at least twenty-one countries from Asia and Africa, people voluntarily participated in this widespread violent protest.[13]

In December 2009, tens of thousands of ordinary people demonstrated passionately in Copenhagen to pressure global leaders into taking drastic steps to prevent global warming from becoming irreversible. These protestors were joined by people from 100 other countries, the overall sentiment[14] being that urgent and radical action needs to be taken to curb global warming as there is no Planet B to go to.

Similar global protests take place at the annual meetings of the World Economic Forum—each year better organised, and more violent. Günter Grass (Nobel Laureate for Literature, 1999) reminds us ominously that: 'You have to understand that hunger is war. No gate can withstand the crush of the hungry'.

All this awareness of social injustice came to a head on 17 December 2010 in Tunisia where hungry, unemployed, and oppressed young people had enough of political leaders (and their business leader cohorts) not listening. This was the start of the Jasmine Revolution (named after the national flower of Tunisia), which changed the socio-political landscape in North Africa and parts of the Middle East in a swift and bloody revolt, organised by way of modern social media technology over which their oppressors had no control.[15]

Listening to these voices of civil protest, do you also hear the same despair, anger and aspirations from history?

Can history repeat itself?

Now, let's listen to voices of eminent business scholars, which can only be heard if you read academic books and journals. In the scholarly tradition, penetrating questions are asked.

Peter Drucker: What is the role of management and business in society?[16]

Drucker argues in 1987 that modern society is a construct of managed organisations to deliver on all their tangible and intangible needs. Such organisations vary from businesses to government services to non-governmental organisations. From this he argues that there is perhaps more management happening outside business than inside. Society increasingly expects business to act as one of their organs—and that management scientists and business leaders will take more than fifty years to figure out what this means in practice. This logic contributes to today's quest for corporate social and environmental responsibility.

Charles Handy: What is a business for?[17]

Handy argues in 2002 that just as a beast lives to eat, so today's business enterprises exist to make profit for the investor. In contrast, just as a human being eats to live, the 'delightful' organisation exists to make a difference to the investor, the employee, the community, and the environment—thus, to deliver sustained prosperity to all stakeholders. This logic contributes to today's quest for stakeholder, instead of shareholder value.

Kenichi Ohmae: What is the end-purpose of a firm's vision?[18]

Ohmae argues in 2005 that before a vision can be formulated, there must be clarity on what end-purpose the vision would serve—to what kind of future will this enterprise contribute? This logic contributes to scenario planning as a powerful strategic planning technique.

C. K. Prahalad: What dominant logic is required to eradicate poverty at the bottom of the human pyramid?[19]

Prahalad argues in 2005 that systemic poverty can only be eliminated by way of empowering the poor to become entrepreneurs through innovative business models. In this way the world's poor living on less than US$2 per day would be reduced from 70 per cent to 30 per cent of the world's population—thus, creating a new market of some 3 billion people! This logic contributes to an increased use of 'bottom of the pyramid' business models.

Thomas Maak and Nicola Pless: What is the role of business leaders?[20]

They argue in 2009 that humanity needs responsible business leaders who also contribute to finding solutions for global problems. This logic contributes to questioning the traditional understanding of leadership responsibility amongst thought leaders today.

In my own research[21], I have found that these questions challenging the raison d'être of business, the dominant business logic, and the role and meaning of business leadership have been largely ignored by mainline business scholars in the twentieth century (see Appendix A). It's only recently that business scholars have picked up courage to debate these questions on open forums and in the public domain. I do not know the reason for this historical culture of silence, but one reason for breaking this silence may be that they have been encouraged by visionary voices from leaders-in-practice—a case of practice leading theory.

But let's now listen to these visionary voices from leaders-in-practice:

Muhammad Yunus (chairman of the Grameen Bank in Bangladesh) received the 2006 Nobel Prize for Peace for 'his efforts to create economic and social development from below'.[22]

In January 2008, Bill Gates addressed the World Economic Forum in Davos on 'creative capitalism' that works both to generate profits and to solve the world's inequalities.[23]

In July 2008, at World Youth Day in Sydney, Pope Benedictus XVI said that 'insatiable consumerism [fuelled by irresponsible marketing] was driving global warming and ecological degradation and destroying human values—a poison that corrodes what is good'.[24]

In January 2009, President Barack Obama said in his inauguration speech that the current state of the global economy is 'a consequence of greed and irresponsibility . . . and a failure to make hard choices'.[25]

In January 2011, Klaus Schwab (Founder and Executive Chairman of the World Economic Forum) said that 'leadership today means navigating a larger, more complex set of issues and more complicated relationships', when he referred to the four key issues defining the new reality in the WEF's *Outlook on the Global Agenda for 2011*[26], namely:

> ➢ Global power shifts: Economic and political power is no longer concentrated in the hands of the developed economies. Emerging markets have become centres of both economic growth and geopolitical decision-making.
> ➢ Economic uncertainty: There is a high degree of volatility and ambiguity across many markets in the short to medium term, which is likely to lead to irrational behaviour on the part of investors.
> ➢ Resource scarcity: The strain of providing for a world with a population heading rapidly towards 7 billion and beyond threatens to undercut growth, create environmental problems, and cause social and political conflict.
> ➢ Institutional weakness: Governments and global institutions that were fragile before the crisis have, by and large, become even more so in the face of global instability, which the world is in no state to withstand.

Voices from the arts

Throughout the ages, art was used to voice concern and to point the way forward amidst the busyness of our times. A good example is Victor Hugo's 1662 novel *Les Misérables*[27] which voiced grotesque injustices due to the absence of liberty, freedom, and fraternity in French Society. Let's listen to and reflect upon the chorus of this novel's musical interpretation:

Do you hear the people sing lost in the valley of the night?
It is a music of a people who are climbing to the light.
For the wretched of the earth there is a flame that never dies.
Even the darkest night will end and the sun will shine.
They will live again in freedom in the garden of the Lord.
They will walk behind the ploughshare, they will put away the sword.
The chain will be broken and all men will have their reward.
Will you join in our crusade? Who will be strong and stand with me?
Somewhere beyond the barricade is there a world you long to see?
Do you hear the people sing? Say, do you hear the distant drums?
It is the future that they bring when tomorrow comes!

It is against this background that it becomes clear that business, societal, and political leaders are indeed listening to ordinary people as well as their own conscience. They may use different arguments, articulate their speeches, and launch their actions from their different realities, but they are all envisioning and already working towards certain elements of a new world that is within their sphere of influence and capability. Whilst this is good, I am disillusioned that an overall vision of what to change to is glaringly missing. Marion, Countess Dönhoff[28] was just as disillusioned about such lack of vision when she called out in 1995 'No one has a vision today. No one can say what should happen or what the long-term future should bring. A sense of helplessness pervades cultural life, and there is an oppressive void'.

From the voices it is clear that humanity calls for change in the way they live and work for the sake of their unborn. It's also clear that humanity is increasingly becoming more holistic in their world view and, with the help of modern social media technology, becoming better organised to make their voice heard—and, they are becoming more assertive to make their aspirations for a better world happen. However, ominously, there is no indication that modern society is going to wait for more than 100 years for change to happen as was the case in the sixteenth and seventeenth century before the French Revolution started.

No wonder, the 2011 Person of the Year award was 'The Protestor'. The *Times Magazine's* annual award recognised the global rise of civil society against political abuse and the consequences of 'hell-bent mega scaled crony hyper capitalism'[29] and called for a new deal . . . a new social contract.

The good news is that the voices from both humanity and their leaders are in agreement that quantum change in the way we live and work is urgently necessary.

Gary Hamel[30], a business scholar, indirectly adds fuel to these voices by saying that the gap between what can be imagined and what can be achieved has never been smaller than today. In other words, if humanity calls for a better world, the means are there to deliver whatever world humanity cares to imagine. Nancy Adler[31], an artist and business scholar, puts this logic in a practical context by asking 'Now that we can do anything, what will we do?'

Listening to this wide variety of voices from around the world, my overwhelming conclusion is that humanity is ready and willing for a change from today's world. Whilst there seems to be agreement on why change is necessary and what needs to change, there is an incomplete view of precisely what the end-game of the change should be.

My question, therefore, is: Change yes, but change to what?

In the next chapter, I will answer this question through inductive reasoning in order to set global leadership in motion towards a common goal—humanity's change mandate to its leaders.

---

[1]   Küng, H. 1998. *A global ethic for global politics and economics.* Oxford: Oxford University Press, page 98.

[2]   Stumpf, E. S. and Abel, D. C. 2002. *Elements of Philosophy: An Introduction*, 4th ed. New York: McGraw Hill.

[3]   The Online Encyclopaedia and Dictionary: www.fact-archive.com/encyclopedia/List_of_countries_by_system_of_government.

[4]   Down, R. B. 2004. *Books that Changed the World. A Signet Classic.*

[5]   http://en.wikipedia.org/wiki/Black_Death.

[6]   www.unep.org/dewa/Portals/67/pdf/Global_Bee_Colony_Disorder_and_Threats_insect_pollinators.pdf.

[7]   Immigration—Why Europe's all at sea. *Time Magazine*, 1 March 2010.

[8]   Neighbour India quietly fencing out Bangladesh. http://seattletimes.nwsource.com/html/nationworld/2003762578_bangfence26.html.

[9]   Illegal immigrants in South Africa [Onwettiges plaas enorme druk op SA]. www.beeld.com 3 March 2010.

[10] *Kosmos Journal.* Taken from various editions between Winter 2008 and Winter 2010.

[11] *Kosmos Journal*, 2008. Making the great adjustment—Coalition for the global commons by James Quiligan. 7(2).

[12] Source: Unknown, but probably from the Bird Clan of the Cherokee.

[13] World food price crisis of 2008-09: http://en.wikipedia.org.

[14] Planet B ['Verander stelsel, nie klimaat' en 'Daar is g'n planeet B' sê betogers]. http://www.beeld.com, 13 December 2009.

[15] *The Times.* 9 February 2011. Class of 2011.

[16] Drucker, P. F. 1987. "Management: the problems of success', *Academy of Management Executive*, 1(1): 13-19.

[17] Handy, C. 2002. 'What's business for?', *Harvard Business Review*, 80(12): 49-55.

[18] Ohmae, K. 2005. *The Next Global Stage: Challenges and Opportunities in Our Borderless World.* Upper Saddle River: Wharton School Publishing, p. 271.

[19] Prahalad, C. K. 2005. *The Fortune at the Bottom of the Pyramid: Eradicating Poverty Through Profits.* Upper Saddle River: Wharton School Publishing.

[20] Maak, T. and Pless, N. M. 2009. Business leaders as citizens of the world—Advancing humanism on a global scale. *Journal of Business Ethics*, 88: 537-550.

[21] Coetzee, J. J. 2009. A social contract with business as the basis for a postmodern MBA in a world of inclusive globalisation—A critical metasynthesis. ISBN 1-59942-290-5 (a published doctoral thesis in business leadership from the University of South Africa).

[22] www.nobelprize.org.

[23] www.gatesfoundation.org/speeches-commentary/Pages/bill-gates-2008-world-economic-forum-creative-capitalism.aspx.

[24] www.vatican.va/holy_father/benedict_xvi/messages/youth/documents/hf_ben-xvi_mes_20070720_youth_en.html.

[25] www.whitehouse.gov/blog/inaugural-address/.

[26] http://www.weforum.org/community/risk-response-network.

[27] The musical by Victor Hugo, *Les Misérables*. A Cameron Macintosh, Royal Shakespeare Company Production.

[28] Gräfin M. Dönhoff, 1995. 'Zehn Thesen', *Die Zeist*, 24 November [as quoted by H. Küng 1998. *A global ethic for global politics and economics.* Oxford: Oxford University Press, p. X11].

[29] *The Times.* 26 December 2011. 2011 person of the Year, pp. 37-68.

[30] Hamel, G. 2000. *Leading the Revolution*. Boston, MA: Harvard University Press, p. 10.

[31] Adler, N. J., 2006. The arts and leadership: Now that we can do anything, what will we do? *Academy of Management and Learning,* 5(4): 486-499.

Note: All references to Nobel laureates—see Appendix B

CHAPTER 2

ACTING ON VOICES FROM AROUND THE WORLD

In this chapter, we examine the voices from around the world through inductive reasoning, and ask what the root causes of these voices are, and what common themes they have.

The root causes will enable us to better understand the messages on the continuum between the voices of angst and the voices of hope. The common themes of the voices will enable us to better understand what it is that humanity yearns for—after all, this is humanity's change mandate to business, societal, and political leaders.

Before we proceed, let's just ensure that we all understand what inductive reasoning means. It's a widely accepted method of reasoning when faced with limited evidence, which suggests a conclusion but cannot confirm one. In the interest of moving a debate or a process forward, a temporary conclusion is made based on the available evidence. It's about taking a temporary chance with the truth! The underlying premise is that when new evidence emerges, the temporary conclusion may have to be adjusted. Such new evidence may arise from new information or from definitive research.

The classic example of inductive reasoning is as follows:

Joe has seen 100 white swans. From inductive reasoning, Joe concludes that all swans are white. This conclusion is valid until one black swan is seen. Thereafter, the next truth is that all swans are either white or black. This new conclusion is only valid until a swan of a different colour is seen or until a definitive research on the colour of all swans from around the world yields a final and indisputable conclusion.

Let's begin by examining only four root causes of the voices. This will be sufficient to build a contextual framework for understanding the messages voiced.

Communism and capitalism, the world's dominant socio-economic delivery systems since World War II (WW II), have collapsed. The collapse of communism was signalled by the fall of the Berlin Wall in 1989, and the collapse of capitalism was signalled by the global economic crisis of 2008, which continued up to 2012 (and probably beyond). Consequently, the core global discourse today is about what economic delivery system could provide both prosperity and a sustained future, with the broad scope of options indicated in Table 2.1.

Table 2.1: A spectrum of economic delivery systems

Premise	Personal freedom		Golden Rule of Humanity	State control	
Core driving force	*Greed for money* 'The Earth is an infinite resource—let's indulge and not think about tomorrow'.		*Global stewardship* 'Unlimited economic and population growth is not possible in a finite world'.	*Greed for power* 'I have supreme knowledge. I know best. Therefore, I will think for you, and will tell you what to do'.	
Economic delivery system	Capitalism	Neo capitalism; Creative capitalism	Eco-economical conservationism	Democratic socialism; Social democracy	Communism State capitalism
← increased probability of corruption and shredding the social contract →					

Source: Berry[1], adapted by the author.

The voices from Chapter 1 call for a kind of eco-economical conservationism[2] is emerging as a probable best-fit economic delivery system. However, further research is required that goes beyond today's popular big ideas such as shared value creation, creative capitalism, responsible capitalism, stakeholder economics, financial inclusion, and The Montfort Plan.[3]

These big ideas help the global discourse on an alternative economic delivery system forward in a positive manner. However, whilst all these big ideas are helpful, none are tried and tested, and none recognise the reality of China's economic miracle over the past twenty years, delivered by state capitalism—a fusion of the worst of capitalism and communism.

The way today's geo-political and socio-economic forces are shaping a new world is comparable to the Industrial Revolution some 200 years ago, according to *The Economist*.[4] The difference is that, two centuries ago, only a third of the global population was affected; today, nearly the entire global population is affected.

A probable future balance of power will have to be found between the developed and the developing worlds. Finding this new balance will not be without immense positive and negative impacts on the way we live, making it even harder for humanity to understand the historical context of its time. Let's take two extreme examples:

> ➢ Will the G3 (USA, European Union, and Japan) give up their power and global market share without a fight by way of radical innovations? Imagine the positive impact on the world of an American economy that is carbon, water, and waste neutral! Now imagine the opposite.

> ➤ Conversely, what will BRICS (Brazil, Russia, India, China, and South Africa) do with their new-found power and increased global market share? Imagine the positive impact on the world if China emerges as a global champion for democracy and civil rights! Now imagine the opposite.

The mindless pursuit of profit by business since WW II has led to a spiritual vacuum, known as 'horror vaccui'.[5] Although he has made technological advances, man has lost his soul in the process. Since he cannot stand this emptiness from within, he has filled it with things only money can buy—as in a religion of greed. This spiritual dysfunctionality is exploited by modern marketing, resulting in a destructive culture of insatiable consumerism.

This spiritual dysfunctionality is further exacerbated by management fallacies promoted by management witchdoctors (masquerading as gurus) who profess that the firm's only success metric is to make profit—thus, the more profit a firm makes, the more socially responsible it becomes. Another fallacy is that a business leader is not a member of society—thus, the schizophrenic mindset of an exploiter by day and fearing the future for his or her children by night!

But let's wait, as these and other fallacies will be fully exposed later in the book.

The last root cause is that a new global landscape is emerging because of powerful impacts. These impacts are hardly noticed on a day-to-day basis, but over time they drive the voices varying from angst to hope. This new global landscape is also the new context of human life, which is now described by way of the well-known PPESTLE model below (for the sake of simplicity, only one positive and negative indicator is given):

A new **P**olitical environment:

> *Positive indicator*: For example, a new balance of global political and economic power, which will bring checks and balances into force as a safeguard for humanity living in the West, East, and South.

> *Negative indicator*: For example, the role of fundamentalism or terror in local, regional, and global politics as a threat to human security.

A new **P**hysical environment:

> *Positive indicator*: For example, the increased global reach of infrastructure, infostructure, and open-source knowledge to all people on Earth.

> *Negative indicator*: For example, Planet Earth's natural resources (its minerals, oil, and gas) and natural ability to sustain life (by its forests, agricultural soil, rivers, fresh water, and biodiversity) are being depleted.

A new **E**conomic environment:

> *Positive indicator*: For example, a new economic delivery system to replace capitalism is being called for by all responsible global leaders.

> *Negative indicator*: For example, the all-pervasive destructive influence of global crime (arguably the world's third largest economy).

A new **S**ocial environment:

> *Positive indicator*: For example, an increased awareness of global threats and that all humanity shares the same fate.

> *Negative indicator*: For example, the exponential growth in human population and uncontrolled human migration.

A new **T**echnological environment:

> *Positive indicator*: For example, all technologies have already been developed to address today's 'threats without borders' and global commons issues.

> *Negative indicator*: For example, a lack of political will to creatively roll out today's technology for the benefit of humanity.

A new **L**egal or institutional environment:

> *Positive indicator*: For example, it is generally accepted that global institutions need to change—today's global debate is about *how*, and not *if*.

> *Negative indicator*: For example, no ability to enforce global accountability or international law.

A new **E**cological environment:

> *Positive indicator*: For example, a global recognition that man's negative influence on the environment must be curtailed urgently.

Negative indicator: For example, resistance to change to a green economy due to vested interests.

Understanding the new context for human life as described above enables us to better understand the interdependent and interrelated root causes of the angst and hope contained in the voices from around the world. I hope that this better understanding will create higher levels of awareness and empathy about the kind of world that humanity yearns for, and consequently a new understanding of the role and meaning of business leadership and business as an organ of society.

Let's now begin to examine precisely what it is that humanity longs for.

Given the advances of global information communication technology (e.g., television and the Internet), socialisation (e.g., blogs and Facebook) and open knowledge domains (e.g., Wikipedia and Google), it is as though humanity is discovering itself for the first time. Today, people from around the world realise that they share the same values and aspire to the same things such as a happy, safe, and clean environment as well as access to food, shelter, energy, health, education, and opportunity. They also realise that they all share the same fate from the same 'threats without borders'.

People from the West, East, and South, today, realise that if they stand together they can do something about their joint fate and their joint aspirations. For the first time in history, someone from

Peru has something in common with someone from Pakistan, Papua New Guinea, Poland, or Puerto Rico. Two recent examples of this new-found human solidarity are the global protests over high food prices in 2008 and the spread of political unrest in North African and Middle East countries in 2010/11.

But what is the common theme that ordinary people talk about in Canada, Cameroon, Chile, China, and Cyprus? What is the agenda of this new conversation amongst humanity discovering itself for the first time? Is there an appropriate framework to understand this new conversation amongst people from the West, East, and South?

Global Trends 2015: A dialogue about the future with nongovernmental experts provides such an appropriate conversational framework because it's credible, transparent, inclusive, and written in practical leadership language.

This unclassified study[6], commissioned by the American National Intelligence Council, provides a flexible framework for long-term strategic planning and debate. The study also provides insight into the probable future of global socio-economic and geo-political deflection points, which will ultimately shape a post-WW II world order. Its scenario planning is based on the following assumptions: (a) American global influence will wane, (b) moderate but steady economic growth is required, and (c) countries negatively affected by population growth, resource scarcity, and bad governance are prone to internal conflict and state failure.

Before we proceed, let's just make sure we all understand what scenario planning is all about. Scenario planning is a strategy decision-making tool to identify probable futures for a firm, industry, or country. Typically, two key variables that will shape the future of the firm are identified and plotted as the X-axis and the Y-axis of a scenario game board. Depending how these two variables unfold, four probable futures emerge. The strategic challenge is then to identify through analysis and reasoning where the firm is currently (today's world), and where it wants to be (their ideal world). The growth-path from today's world to the ideal world provides the context for the firm's vision and strategy implementation—that is, working towards an ideal end-state.

To illustrate this, let's take an example of two competing firms with the same vision, namely, 'To be world class producer of printing paper'. Firm A's end-purpose is make money, the more the better—that's their ideal future world. Firm B's end-purpose is to make a sustained difference to all stakeholders—that's their ideal future world. From this simple example, it is clear that the two firms will act entirely different in the marketplace, despite having the same vision statement.

When interpreting *Global Trends 2015s* findings in scenario planning logic (see Figure 2.1), there are two mutually exclusive variables that will ultimately shape the world of tomorrow:

X-axis: the extent of humanity's broad security; and

Y-axis: the extent to which globalisation eradicates systemic poverty.

Figure 2.1: World order scenario game board

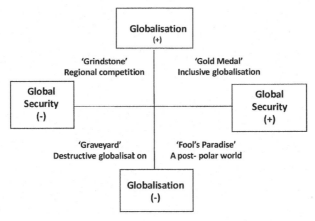

+: The best that can reasonably be achieved   X-axis: Continuum of human security
-: The worst that can reasonable be imagined   Y=axis: Continuum of human poverty

Source: *Global Trends 2015*[7], with metaphors from Sunter[8].

Depending on the ratio in which these two key variables may unfold in future, four probable world orders emerge, namely, regional competition, destructive globalisation, a post-polar world, or inclusive globalisation. For the sake of completeness, all four global scenarios are described in detail in Appendix A.

Each of these probable future world scenarios would produce a distinctly different society with its own unique way of doing life and work, metaphorically depicted as Gold Medal, Fool's Paradise, Grindstone, and Graveyard kind of societies (see Figures 2.1). To illustrate these metaphors, let's picture the plight of children living in the Graveyard and the Gold Medal worlds by contrasting their reality below, and also in Figure 4.1:

Graveyard	Gold Medal
Blank eyes	Shining eyes
Anxious	Content
Underfed	Well nourished
Diseased	Healthy
No education	Good education
Hopeless	A future

The voices from Chapter 1 indicate that humankind yearns for the Gold Medal scenario, where prosperity and stability are the norm and one can live a happy and purposeful life (e.g., the universal needs of humankind as envisaged by Aristotle [384-322 BC] and Plutarchus [AD 46-120]). Such a state of being can only be achieved with the Golden Rule of Humanity as the glue that binds humanity together.

Such a state of being is not another dreamtime Utopia. There is much evidence that a trend towards a world order of inclusive globalisation (WOIG) is already emerging, that is, the Gold medal scenario. Let's examine this evidence by reflecting on the life experience of two Nobel laureates:

Regarding the *Y-axis* of the WOIG, Muhammad Yunus makes a case for developing poor people in a sustained manner, namely, to give them the opportunity to become consumers as well as producers of goods and services. In his acceptance speech of the Nobel Prize for Peace in 2006, he said: 'Poor people are bonsai people. There is nothing wrong in their seeds. Simply, society never gave them the base to grow on. All it needs to get the poor people out of poverty is for us to create an enabling environment for them. Once the poor can unleash their energy and creativity, poverty will disappear very quickly.'

Regarding the *X-axis* of the WOIG, Al Gore makes a case for responsible business models and government policies to advance human security. In his acceptance speech of the Nobel Prize for Peace in 2007, he said: 'A goal in our modern world must be to maintain human security in the broadest sense. This includes security arising from the adverse impacts of environmental degradation on society, such as access to clean water, access to sufficient food, stable health conditions, ecosystem resources . . .'

Further evidence that a WOIG is already emerging comes from two eminent scholars working in completely different fields of knowledge.

Professor Ervin Lazlo[9], a leading figure in systems philosophy and general evolution theory, theorised that human society is starting to shift from a *logos civilisation* to a *holos civilisation*. The characteristic of a *logos civilisation* is a short-term mentality that produces more negative social, economic, and ecological side effects than positive achievements. The characteristic of a *holos civilisation* is a harmonious human or nature interface in a systemic whole.

All voices calling for holism, sustainability, and the security of humanity would broadly fall into the sphere of a holos civilisation, as indicated by the *X-axis* of the global scenario game board—that is, the extent to which security can be delivered to humanity through business models.

Professor C. K. Prahalad, a leading figure in business science, convincingly argued that poverty can be eradicated profitably. Around 70 per cent of humankind lives in a state of systemic poverty, earning less than US$2 per day. He asked why we ignore the world's biggest market of some three billion people, and proposed to enter this market through a wealth-creation process he called the second wave of globalisation. This is a unique wealth-creation process that rolls out all the benefits of today's first wave of globalisation to the top 30 per cent of the human pyramid to the bottom 70 per cent of the human pyramid in order to eradicate poverty in a sustained manner.

All voices calling for fairness, justice, and reaching out to the poor would broadly fall in this sphere, as indicated by the *Y-axis* of the global scenario game board—that is, the extent to which poverty can be eliminated through the second wave of globalisation.

The bottom line impact of what humanity wants is a radical transformation in the shape of the human pyramid: from a triangle in a WODG to that of a diamond shape in a WOIG as illustrated in Figure 2.2.

Figure 2.2: A radically altered shape of the human pyramid

Through the second wave of globalisation, the shape of the human pyramid is changed from a triangle to a diamond. This would create the world's largest new market of 3 billion people, currently living on less than US$2/day!

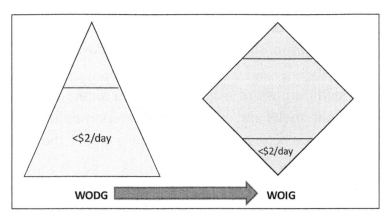

Source: C. K. Prahalad[10].

Using inductive reasoning, I now conclude that the root cause of the voices from Chapter 1 is that humanity wants to move away from a world scenario of destructive globalisation. The common theme is that a WOIG is worth aspiring to as an alternative. Consequently, the temporary conclusion is that humanity has given a mandate to its leaders, which can be summarised as follows:

Humanity's global sustainability mandate to its business, societal, and political leaders:

> *To lead humanity away from today's world of destructive globalisation to a world of inclusive globalisation.*

Such a leadership mandate calls for a dual growth-path, progressing simultaneously along the *X-axis* to increase humanity's broad security, and the *Y-axis* to eliminate systemic poverty through inclusive globalisation.

This duality in humanity's global sustainability mandate cuts to the core of today's business leadership dilemmas, namely:

➢ The kind of economic delivery system that can deliver on both success criteria;
➢ The role, responsibility, and purpose of business leadership in society;
➢ The end-purpose of a firm's vision, business models, and corporate social and environmental responsibilities; and
➢ The balance between the local and the global, the short and the long term.

Humanity seems to respond to the above dilemmas by simply saying to business leaders: 'deal with your own dilemmas, but deliver our global sustainability mandate because the burden of our poverty and insecurity is unbearable—listen to, and act upon our voices!'

———

I can hear you say: 'This mandate comes from inductive reasoning—you have taken a chance with the truth!'

I agree, but in order to move our dialogue forward I had to take a chance with the truth to come to a temporary conclusion. The implications of this mandate are so awesome that it must be verified by way of robust and trustworthy research.

In the next chapter a research methodology will be designed to prove or disprove the temporary conclusion that humanity has mandated its leaders to deliver a WOIG.

---

1   Berry, A. J. 1997. Approaching the millennium-transforming leadership education for stewardship of the planet's resources. *Leadership and Organisation Development Journal*, 45(5): 86-92. [Simplified and expanded by the Author].

2   Economic Conservationism is described by Wogaman, 1977. *Christians and the Great Economic Debate*. London: SCM Press.

3   Pozuelo-Montfort, J. 2010. *The Montfort Plan: The New Architecture of Capitalism*. New York: Wiley.

4   The Economist. 16 September 2006. 'The new titans: a survey of the world economy', pp. 3-34.

5   Küng, H. 1998. *A Global Ethic for Global Politics and Economics*. Oxford: Oxford University Press, p. 274.

6   Global Trends 2015 states in the covering letter from the Director of Central Intelligence: 'We intended to make GT-2015 an unclassified assessment to be shared with the public'. In the Chairman of the national Intelligence Council's covering letter it is stated: 'The DT-2015 should be seen as a work in progress—a flexible framework for thinking about the future . . . we welcome comments on all aspects of this study.'

7   *Global trends 2015: a dialogue about the future with non-governmental experts*. 2000. USA National Intelligence Council Report.

8   *Clem Sunter*. www.mindofafox.com.

9   Laszlo, E. 2006. *Paths to a Planetary Civilisation*, 6(2). www.kosmosjournal.org.

10   Prahalad, C. K. 2005. *The Fortune at the Bottom of the Pyramid: Eradicating Poverty*. Upper Saddle River: Wharton School Publishing.

PART 2

A RESEARCH-BASED ANSWER

From David Gross (Nobel Laureate for Physics, 2004)

'The more we know, the more we are aware of what we do not know. The questions we ask today are more profound . . . because we are intelligently ignorant today. I am happy to report that there is no evidence that we are running out of our most important resource—ignorance.'

CHAPTER 3

HARVESTING WISDOMS FROM AROUND THE WORLD

The objective of this chapter is to provide a layman's introduction to the research methodology used to discover what it is that humanity yearns for. Change, yes, but to what?

By way of inductive reasoning, I have concluded at the end of Chapter 2 that humanity's global sustainability mandate to its leaders is to deliver a WOIG. Remember that this mandate comes from taking a chance with the truth. Before moving any further, I need more proof that this mandate is representative, unbiased, credible, and realistic. Thought leaders would ask if this mandate is real and whether it could be implemented. Researchers would ask if this mandate is trustworthy.

When looking for an appropriate research methodology within my own field of expertise, I was mortified to discover that no existing research methodology was capable to discover new knowledge at the intersection of various knowledge domains. As you will appreciate, the temporary conclusion about humanity's global sustainability mandate spans at least across the domains of management, economics, philosophy, education, social, and earth sciences, that is, it's not confined to the traditional narrow context of business science. This sad reality motivated me to *invent* a new research methodology.

However, from the beginning of the invention process I was haunted by the question: How can a fair and reasonable construct of our leaders' collective wisdom be obtained? Thankfully, I was guided by two philosophical principles, which state as follows:

To deal with the full truth: Here, I was reminded by the business scientist, Ivor Ansoff[1] who said that you should start researching at the highest possible level. In this way you are hedged against mistaking a half-truth as the full truth. For this reason, I have started with the highest possible research question, namely, 'What kind of future does humanity want?'

To deal with reality: Here, I was reminded by the educational philosopher, Parker Palmer, who said[2], 'Moments when illusion is stripped away and reality is revealed are extremely hard to come by. There is a vast conspiracy against them [to reveal reality]'. For this reason, the sample of Global Icons (see Appendix B) was selected by way of pre-designed selection criteria to weed out any personal bias. In this way, I had no control over the actual individuals selected. In order to weed out any illusion, I researched the Global Icon's answers to the Socratic questions by analysing their official speeches—that is, without asking them specific questions. In this way illusion had been stripped away from me and that of the Global Icons, and consequently reality emerged.

Armed with this wisdom, I set off on an intellectual safari to discover a paradigm-busting research methodology, which I termed *critical metasynthesis.* Figure 3.1 depicts the overall research process, which is a unique combination of the following well-known research methodologies:

> ➢ *Metasynthesis* integrates and interprets the results of different, but related studies. Its outcome is a model or trends of similar meaning (i.e., phenomena);

> *Trustworthiness* is the ultimate criterion for quality interpretive research. This calls for compliance with fifty-three quality assurance criteria to demonstrate academic rigour and trustworthiness of the metasynthesis;

> *Socrates' method of systematic inquiry* seeks the truth by finding answers to questions for which the questioner does not know. This is done by probing towards the truth in an increasingly focused (or funnelled) manner, so that the next question arises from the answer to the previous question; and

> *Critical management research* challenges the status quo to provide new boundaries, new paradigms, or new agendas by way of three loosely structured intellectual steps, namely, to gain insight (i.e., metasynthesis), to critique the insight (i.e., deconstruction), and to re-define the critiqued insight (i.e., transformative redefinition).

Figure 3.1 The overall research process

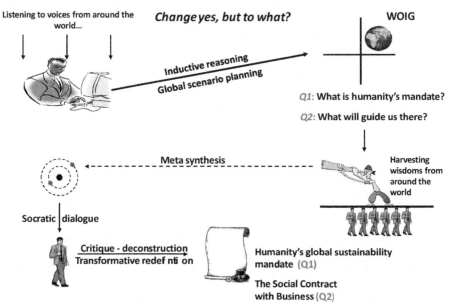

Source: Author; clip art from Microsoft Word.

Let me now explain the three intellectual steps in the critical management research method in such a way that you are comfortable with the manner in which humanity's global sustainability mandate to its leaders is proved or disproved.

The first step is a series of design criteria that will yield a trustworthy **insight** into the wisdom from today's leaders representing humanity:

> ➢ Leadership types: I selected business, societal, and political leaders because any new world—and, consequently any new context for business—will be shaped individually and collectively by them.
> ➢ Representativeness: I selected the G3 countries (representing some forty per cent of global wealth and fifteen per cent of the global population) and the BRICS countries (representing some fifteen per cent of global wealth and forty per cent of the global population). Respectively, they are considered representative of the developed and the developing world in the West, East, and South. Collectively, the G3 and the BRICS counties represent 55 per cent of global wealth and also 55 per cent of the global population.
> ➢ Leader's names: I did not select any specific individual, but have only set the following selection criteria for each country in the G3 and BRICS—namely, for business leaders: the chairpersons of the two public listed firms with the highest market capitalisation in each country; for social leaders: the rector and dean of the largest university and business school respectively in each country; and for political leaders: the current and immediate past president in each country—indeed, a formidable selection of powerful positions which provide leaders with the means and power to change the world.

> The Socratic questions were as follows but prompted by eminent scholars[3,4,5,6,7,8,9]:

What kind of future does humanity want? What is the nature of this new world that humanity is yearning for, and what is its dynamics?

What kind of society can deliver and sustain such a future? It is clear that a new kind of society needs to arise, with a different value system and new ways of doing life.

What kind of business will such a society require? It is clear that a new value proposition for business needs to be found. This new kind of society is a construct of a multitude of organisations that provide for people's livelihood and support services. Business is one such construct of society. The others are civil and government organisations, which are increasingly being managed along professional management and business principles to increase the quality of service delivery to society.

What kind of leader will such a business require? It is clear that a new role and meaning for leadership is required to lead a business as an organ of society. The same applies to leaders who lead civil and government organisations in a business-like manner.

> Credible sources of information: I selected only official public domain speeches of the selected global leaders to find their answers to the Socratic questions. I also selected commentary from lead articles in the Economist and the Financial Times on the selected global leaders.

The second intellectual step is to **critique** the wisdoms from the global leaders. For this, I needed a formidable and trustworthy control group to refute and/or to add value to the wisdoms from the global leaders. I decided to use all the Nobel laureates over a ten-year period as the control group. All the Nobel laureates (peace, economics, literature, and science) have been selected by Swedish institutes—that is, their selection had been done independently from my research. They are all honoured for their acts of wisdom, love, and courage resulting in new trends, new paradigms, and confronting injustices. In fact, they offer the best humanity has to offer from around the world. I decided to use their formal presentation and acceptance Nobel Prize speeches to also find answers to the same Socratic questions asked to the global leaders as depicted in Figure 3.2.

Figure 3.2 Structure of Global Icons and Socratic questions

Source: Author.

The third intellectual step is to **redefine** the critiqued insight. Doing this, I relied on my own 'body of knowledge', which is my broad education (thirteen years of tertiary education), my lived experience as a business executive (thirty years), and as a business scholar (ten years). I was also guided by the thinking of some of the most influential academics in business leadership—see Appendix C for a list of more than 100 scholarly contributions, which collectively represent at least a century of independent research from eminent scholars from around the world. This incredible mountain of wisdom, research, and lived experience made me as humble as it must have been for Sir Isaac Newton's[10] when he said, after publishing his *Principia Mathematica* in 1687, 'If I have seen farther than other men, it is by standing on the shoulders of giants.'

Harvesting wisdoms from around the world was done over an eight-year period, and in two phases, namely, (a) firstly, formal research in business leadership between 2005 and 2008; and (b) secondly, continuously updating the formal research from 2009 to 2011 for the purpose of this book.

In the next chapter, I will introduce the Socratic dialogue with Global Icons to find a robust and trustworthy answer to the question: change, yes, but to what?

For the academic reader: My research monograph[11] may be obtained from any bookstore of note. It is not re-published here, given the specialised nature thereof.

In this research monograph you will find the literature review, the antecedents, the research design, and the outcomes of the research (Figure 3.3).

Figure 3.3 Critical metasynthesis—the overall knowledge creation process

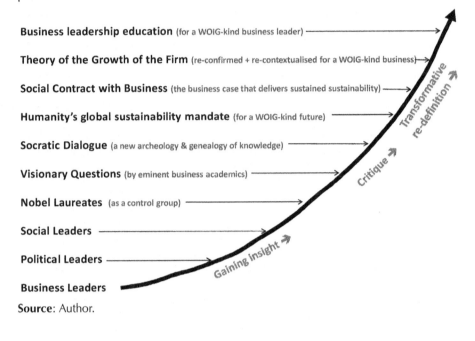

Source: Author.

1 Ansoff, H. I. 1980. 'Strategic issue management', *Strategic Management Journal,* 1(2): 131-148.

2 Palmer, P. J. 1990. *The Creative Life—A Spirituality of Work, Creativity, and Caring.* New York: Harper Row. p. 26 [quoted by Nancy J. Adler. 2006: The arts and leadership: Now that we can do anything, what will we do? *Academy of Management and Learning,* 5 (4): 486-499].

3 Ohmae, K. 2005. *The Next Global Stage: Challenges and Opportunities in Our Borderless World.*

4 Laszlo, E. 2006. *Paths to a Planetary Civilisation,* 6(2). <www.kosmosjournal.org/> (Accessed on 6 November 2006).

5 Brugmann, J. and Prahalad, C. K. 2007. Cocreating business's new social compact. *Harvard Business Review,* February: 80-90.

6   Berry, A. J. 1997. 'Approaching the millennium: Transforming leadership education for stewardship of the planet's resources', *Leadership and Organisation Development Journal*, 45(5): 86-92.

7   Hart, S. L. 1997. 'Beyond greening: Strategies for a sustainable world', *Harvard Business Review*, Jan/Feb: 67-76.

8   Drucker, P. F. 1987. 'Management: The problems of success', *Academy of Management Executive*, 1(1): 13-19.

9   Prahalad, C. K. 2005. *The Fortune at the Bottom of the Pyramid: Eradicating Poverty Through Profits*. Upper Saddle River: Wharton School Publishing.

10 Sir Isaac Newton reflecting on his book, *Principia Mathematica* in 1687: Robert B. Downs. 2004. Books that changed the world. Signet Classics, p. 211. In this book he laid the foundations for most of today's laws of motion in science, engineering, and technology.

11 Coetzee, J. J. 2009. A social contract with business as the basis for a postmodern MBA in a world of inclusive globalisation—A critical metasynthesis. ISBN 1-59942-290-5 (a published doctoral thesis in business leadership from the University of South Africa).

CHAPTER 4

A SOCRATIC DIALOGUE WITH GLOBAL ICONS

The objective of this chapter is to synthesise the 1,000 plus wisdoms from the Global Icons into a Socratic dialogue in order to:

> ➤ verify humanity's global sustainability mandate; and, if positive
> ➤ to describe this mandate in business leadership language; and
> ➤ to identify the strategic building blocks required to deliver this mandate.

In order to achieve the above objectives, the Socratic dialogue will be structured as follows:

The participants: Socrates, global leader (as spokesperson for all the business, societal, and political leaders), Nobel laureate (as spokesperson for all the Nobel laureates), and myself as the author.

To gain insight: The global leader answers Socrates' specific question by synthesizing the respective themes of wisdom listed in Appendix B.

To critique the insight: Nobel laureate answers Socrates' specific question by also synthesising the respective themes of wisdom listed in Appendix B. In this way, the Nobel laureate acts as a control group by either refuting or adding value to the global leader's answer.

To redefine the critiqued insight: The author will then transformatively redefine global leader's and the Nobel laureate's answer to each Socratic question.

Writing style: In order to make this research-based chapter reader-friendly, I will use an itemised style of writing to package the large amount of wisdoms and scholarly insights into digestible chunks. I also encourage you to follow this dialogue with patience as the truth unfolds, and also to reflect on the points of wisdom (and foolishness), love (and hate), and courage (and cowardice) made by the Global Icons.

———————

Socrates: What kind of future does humanity want?

Global leader

Currently, human suffering is rife. Around 840 million people do not have enough to eat, while twice the number killed in WW II, die each year of hunger and incurable diseases. These indicators of human suffering clearly call for a new vision for the future.

Hence, my *vision* for the future is a world that is in compliance with the ideals of the United Nations, which represent the values and aspirations of its members—it's the collective ambition of 193 nations!

To achieve this vision, I must strive to deliver on the call of people all over the world to establish an equitable and just political and economic world order to advance peace and the development of humankind. I must work with wisdom and courage to promote democracy, uphold international law, and strive for harmony and peace, as well as respect cultures and the environment.

Nobel laureate

I concur with the global leader's vision for the future.

However, to formulate my own vision of a future for the world, I need a clear understanding of what humanity does not want to become.

In this regard, I need a factual and empathetic understanding of the global interconnectedness of threats to humankind, such as illiteracy, poverty, infectious disease, environmental degradation, armed conflict, organised crime, and terror. All these threats can rightfully be called 'threats without borders'. I also need a factual and empathetic understanding of the injustices that confront humankind. The following is a factual list of such injustices that I am mindful of:

> Three billion people (about 45 per cent of the world's population) live on less than US$2 a day; one billion people (about 15 per cent of the world's population) live on less than US$1 a day, which is considered extreme poverty;

> 60 per cent of the world's population lives on 6 per cent of the world's income;

> 20 per cent of the world's population consumes 80 per cent of the world's resources;

> US$1 trillion is spent globally on armament per annum. Only one per cent of that expenditure could feed the world's poor for a year; and

> The 9/11 act of terror killed 2998 innocent people, and triggered a global war on terror. However, in the Democratic Republic of the Congo, 3.9 million innocent people were killed since

1998 due to political terror [this is the equivalent of about 1,300 9/11s over the past ten years, or a 9/11 every three days] with very little global concern for this human tragedy.

These injustices result in an ever widening divide between rich and poor, powerful and powerless, free and fettered, and other divides in access to information, opportunity, living conditions, education, and health.

Only if I understand the order of magnitude and the human face of the implications of the above injustices, can I begin to think what it is that humanity wants to become.

In the broadest sense, humanity wants a state of sustained human security. To achieve this state of being in our future, it is necessary to reduce military tools, as well as to change the warring heart and mind of humankind. This implies that the leadership challenge is to change humanity's inclination to bellicosity.

Given the reality of grotesque injustices against humanity on the one hand, and the desire for sustained human security on the other hand, my *vision* for the future is simply that countless people should work together in solidarity towards delivery of the United Nation's Millennium Development Goals. Delivery on these goals would address the root causes of unresolved global problems, with sustained human security as the outcome.

Author

Reflecting on the Global Icons' dialogue, I conclude that their answers are mutually supportive. Issues that struck me from their dialogue are:

The global leader and the Nobel laureate both leveraged their vision from the ideals and action plans formulated by the United Nations. I am surprised at the high level of consensus on the short-term viability of this vision, given that only a few countries would be able to meet the UN's Millennium Development Goals.

However, none of the Global Icons envisaged that all countries in the world would comply 100 per cent with the ideals and action plans of the United Nations; they spoke of the ideal end-state vision for the future. In reality, all countries would be in various stages of their own journey towards that end-state vision—just think of the contrast between Sweden and Zimbabwe today.

The Nobel laureate reminded the global leader of the unintended consequences of their leadership, such as poverty and injustice. Is this a leadership blind spot—not to understand the holistic consequences of business models as depicted in Figures 2.1 and 4.1?

Figure 4.1 The human face of business models along the X and Y axes of global scenarios

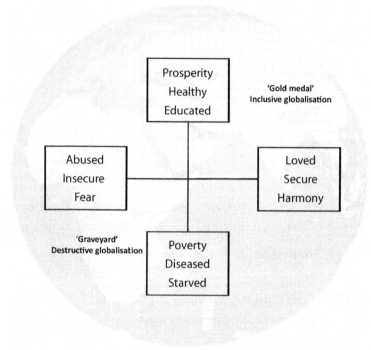

Source: Author.

The various examples of what humanity wants indicate that there is an emerging collective vision of the kind of future that needs to replace today's world. Also, that society is discovering their collective will is a powerful global force for change. And, that society is getting impatient with their leaders for not getting the message of the kind of world they want. Global civil activism is a new reality!

Although their overviews on the current state of the world were not intended to be complete, I missed examples of the order of magnitude of the 'threats without borders'. Only if you know the statistics, you can begin to comprehend the grotesque threat it poses. As an example, let's look at the size of global crime which is estimated to be 10 per cent of global GDP[1]. This means that global crime represents the world's third largest economy after those of the USA and the EU! Why is this anomaly not a generally known fact to society—let alone economists and business schools? Is this a leadership blind spot—to ignore the reality of the context within which global business is done?

I also missed reference to the exponential expansion of the global population from 6.6 billion to 9.2 billion between 2005 and 2050[2]. This is a global ethical and spatial catastrophe that is largely being ignored, or perhaps not understood by today's Global Icons. Is this another leadership blind spot—to ignore the tough challenges facing global leadership?

If nothing is done about the growing injustice facing humanity, a rebellion against tyranny and oppression seems inevitable. This happened with the French Revolution in France around 200 years ago, and has been repeated in many countries since then, when people stood up for their freedom. Or, heaven forbid, will humanity willingly sacrifice its rights, values, and freedoms for state capitalism in a post-democratic world[3], such as China's duality of communist rule and capitalism?

It is clear that the grotesque injustices facing humanity need to be better communicated to decision-makers. Given the complex and overwhelming nature of global statistics, a simple 'global dashboard' to measure the state of justice or injustice to humanity may be a solution.

The visions of a future world given by the Global Icons underpin and echo the voices calling for change in Chapter 1. They also confirm the inductive reasoning for selecting the world order of inclusive globalisation from *Global Trends 2015* as discussed in Chapter 2.

Given the above, my transformative redefinition of the Global Icons' joint vision for the future world is: *a world order of inclusive globalisation (WOIG), where systemic poverty has been permanently removed and where humanity's broad security is assured.*

This is humanity's global sustainability mandate.

This mandate is unambiguous, easy-to-understand, and powerful. In practical terms, this would mean that an American, an Argentinean, an Angolan, and an Australian would have precisely the same understanding of what needs to be achieved as the end-result of their respective action plans to deliver a WOIG-kind future.

Therefore, a WOIG-kind future must be seen as the *kosoryoku* (i.e., the end-result) of humanity's global sustainability mandate, but:

- ➢ without any room for professional, cultural, or scientific misunderstandings;
- ➢ without any room for simplistic slogans, mantras, or formulas to deal with complex interconnected global problems;
- ➢ without any room for business, societal, and political leaders to work against each other; and
- ➢ without any room to sacrifice humanity's values and freedoms when selecting a new economic delivery system to replace today's communism and capitalism.

The following *kairos* events are prerequisites to deliver this WOIG-kind future:

(1) An understanding of the current state of the world in terms of statistics and universal values.

(2) A personal ethic of responsibility towards the future (i.e., global stewardship).

(3) To understand the holistic and intergenerational consequences of business models on poverty and the broad security of society (i.e., conscience-based decision-making).

(4) Improved global communication about the state of the world, as well as the positive and negative trends thereof (i.e., a kind of a global dashboard).

Socrates: What kind of society will build and sustain this kind of future?

Global leader

A kind of society that finds its greatness in humanity, not bellicosity.

The key *values* of such a kind of society would resonate with a society that is democratic; is just, fair, and equitable; is peaceful, stable, and with reduced inequality; has no discrimination on the basis of gender, race, religion, class, or heritage; is drug-free; is secure in terms of basic human needs and physical security; is moderately and sustainably prosperous; is God-fearing; and is prepared to stand up for its values, rights, and aspirations.

This kind of society would produce political leaders who would come forward to serve the people's needs through efficient administration; wise policy development and implementation; making hard choices; and, working within democratic rules.

Regarding the *obstacles*, I propose that we focus on the following:

The first obstacle is sociological deficiencies in society, such as a culture of entitlement, extremism, casteism, xenophobia, intolerance, radicalism, racism, and groups that use terror to stop the advance of democracy.

Such a dysfunctional society would certainly spawn the development of an abusive political system characterised by political leadership deficiencies, which promote self-interest and *nomenklatura* capitalism (where ex-party political *apparatchiks* emerge as instant billionaires), and the foolish pursuit of failed economic systems and failed ideologies. The leadership challenge would be to build trust between society and its political leaders in order to turn around the negative spiral towards the dark.

The next obstacle is leaders who cannot make inclusive decisions about 'threats without borders'. The leadership challenge would be to get rich and poor countries, as well as business, societal, and political leaders to work together towards one inclusive problem-solving process.

Another obstacle is societies that are marginalised by the pace and demands of a globalized world. They are left behind in a state of ignorance, confusion, being resentful, and being poor—the ideal breeding ground for global terror and fundamentalism. The leadership challenge would be to find the balance between being world class while retaining local values, traditions, and knowledge.

The last obstacle is the segmentation of knowledge. Whilst specialization is good, it leads to narrow mindedness and linear thinking. We need to rediscover the value of a broad education. The leadership challenge would be to find new educational paradigms to cultivate a holistic understanding of knowledge and to foster social, cultural, and ecological intelligence.

Regarding the *building blocks*, I would like to encourage the following programmes:

> ➢ To build a modern robust economy. The core driving forces should be communities feeling safe and secure, entrepreneurship, and the bottom of the human pyramid fully participating.
> ➢ To benefit from global learning. This building block is based on global inter-connectedness, collaborative strategies on country, firm and personal levels, as well as the ongoing pursuit of global best practice.
> ➢ To restore social trust after a prolonged period of leadership failures. The leadership tools for this are: to lead by example and with integrity, quality communication, improved policy efficiency, improved service delivery, and to strengthen gatekeeper institutions to check and curb abuse of political power.

Nobel laureate

I agree with the global leader's view that a WOIG kind society needs to find its greatness in humanity, not bellicosity. But the WOIG will not happen unless society has a well functioning, modern, robust, and globally inter-connected economy. This will not happen without courageous leadership. In this regard, I am reminded of Kim Dae-jung's courage to 'fight the intruder' when he said, 'I used all my strength to resist the dictatorial regimes, because there was no other way to defend the people and promote democracy. I felt like a homeowner whose house was invaded by a robber. I had to fight the intruder with my bare hands to protect my family and property without thinking of my own safety'. In praise of his courageous initiative to get the good going in South Korea, the following poem from Gunnar Roaldvam[4] was read at his Nobel Peace Award ceremony in 2000:

> *Once upon a time there were two drops of water;*
> *One was the first, the other the last.*
> *The first drop was the bravest.*
> *I could quite fancy being the last drop,*
> *the one that makes everything run over,*
> *so that we get our freedom back.*
> *But who wants to be the first drop?*

I agree with the global leader's view of society's key values, but would like to state them slightly differently, namely, that the key societal values are found in a society that is protective of its fundamental human rights, which are deeply rooted in religious beliefs.

The fundamental human rights I have in mind are: respect for the individual's dignity—including the dignity of women, children, and the marginalised; respect for the individual's desire for peace, freedom, democracy, tolerance, and justice; and respect for the three laws of human nature—the right to possession, its transfer by consent, and the delivery of promises.

The deeply rooted religious values I have in mind are: the pursuit of a balanced lifestyle, reaching out to one's neighbour, sharing wealth, strong family ties, religious tolerance, stewardship in order to pass on a healthy world to the next generation, and a mindset of 'work is love made visible'.

Regarding *obstacles,* I would like to propose to focus on this: the reasons why civil society is passive, silent and tolerant of injustice;

the lack of holistic thinking amongst leaders and decision-makers; not knowing how to decommission the tools and mindsets of war; not understanding the poor; and poor communication.

Regarding the *building blocks*, I would like to encourage the following programmes:

> ➤ To craft and build a well-functioning and robust economy to deliver long-term prosperity.
> ➤ To cultivate a new generation of mentors and icons who can inspire others to join the turn-around to a WOIG.
> ➤ To cultivate a society-wide global mindset in order to understand the global interconnectedness of all things and the impact thereof on society.
> ➤ To cultivate a society-wide culture of tolerance, respect, and reaching out.
> ➤ To develop wise and courageous leaders who can balance conflicting demands from diverse stakeholders.
> ➤ To build a global network of WOIG-minded individuals and leaders who can support each other, learn from each other, and inspire each other.
> ➤ To build strong democratic structures, with institutional guarantees to protect societal values.
> ➤ To develop financial incentives for business leaders to apply WOIG values, like the carbon exchange market, to deliver a clean living environment.

Author

Reflecting on the Global Icons' dialogue, I conclude that both desire a kind of society that finds its greatness in humanity, and in protecting it by fighting 'the intruder'—a case of a humane society with teeth!

Issues that struck me from their dialogue are:

> That societal values need to drive political and economic systems for sustained positive results. This need not be a surprise, because this is precisely what John Locke said in his social contract theory, which is at the core of today's democracy. However, the reverse seems to be the norm: politicians shred the social contract as they please, and business models dictate human behaviour. The notion of 'society as an organ of business', or 'society as an organ of government' is repulsive and ominous. No wonder global civil activism is on the rise!

> How incapable the communist and capitalist economic delivery systems are of delivering sustained positive results for society! No wonder, the core global discourse today is about what economic delivery system needs to replace failed systems.

> The importance of understanding the interconnectedness of issues in today's globalized world. Yet today the educational focus is on specialization for the sake of qualifying for a job title in the shortest possible time. How much damage is being done by confusing skills training with education? No wonder, much of today's society has lost its soul while pursuing technological excellence.

> The importance of implementation excellence to make societal aspirations and the visions of Global Icons happen. Yet implementation is one of the most neglected subjects in business schools.

> The importance of a religious anchor in society—articulated as a reverence for God by followers of the Abrahamic religions, and reverence for the 'light' or the 'good' by others. The Golden

Rule of Humanity calls for an ethic of personal responsibility, a conscience, and to act in ways that make a positive difference. Sadly, those individuals and societies who have lost their moral compass drive illegal and unethical businesses, which are at the core of a WODG. They will certainly be a formidable force of resistance to change to a WOIG.

When a society experiences broad security, the power of the virtuous cycle brings forth sustained prosperity, education, and the blooming of values that resonate with the Golden Rule of Humanity, such as joy, patience, kindness, goodness, faithfulness, humility, and self-control.

The Global Icons make no mention of the role of labour unions in society. Instead they refer to societal organisations in broad terms only, and probably consider labour unions as only one such civil gatekeeper organisation.

The acknowledgement that the entrepreneurial spirit will always triumph over the bureaucratic spirit is indicative that the future will be driven by entrepreneurs, intrepreneurs, and people of an independent and 'crealistic' mind (a 'crealistic' mind is my own term for those gifted individuals who can dream in creative, yet realistic terms—thus setting the entrepreneurial or innovation process in motion).

Business leaders need a much better understanding of their role in society as well as the wide spectrum of the drivers of a healthy society. Sadly, it is only since the beginning of the twenty-first century that business schools have woken up to this gap in their curriculum. Why did business schools ignore the Ford Foundation's suggestion to include sociology in the MBA curriculum[5] for sixty years? The tragic outcome of this omission is three generations of business leaders with a blind spot about the business/society interface. I was struck by the devastating effect of insatiable consumerism (a core driver of business success) on society when I remembered the voice of Pope Benedictus XVI from Chapter 2 stating 'that insatiable consumerism [fuelled by irresponsible marketing] was driving global warming and ecological degradation and destroying human values—a poison that corrodes what is good'. Table 4.1 indicates the poisonous effect of insatiable consumerism on society. The leadership challenge is to develop business models that do not rely on insatiable consumerism. For such an innovation a new business language and new business success criteria are required.

Table 4.1: What is so bad about consumerism?

What human values are being destroyed by this *poison—insatiable consumerism?*
According to Tim Kasser, there is a strong positive correlation between materialism and several mental and physical maladies. In other words, people who pursue money and things at the expense of relationships and other meaningful endeavours are more likely to suffer from the following 19 problems:

1. Depression	11. Poor impulse control
2. Envy and jealousy	12. Poor physical health
3. Feelings of being controlled	13. Poor self-actualization
	14. Short attention span
4. Feelings of social alienation	15. Shorter, more conflicted relationships
	16. Substance abuse
5. Less desire for equality	17. Social anxiety
6. Less enjoyment of daily activities	18. Tendency to treat others as objects for personal gain
7. Less generosity	19. Unhappiness
8. Mistrust of others	
9. Narcissism	
10. Passive-aggressiveness	

Imagine a country where the entire population suffers from these disorders!
Now imagine the opposite!

Source: Kasser[6], adapted by the author.

Given the above, my transformative redefinition of a WOIG kind of society is that it should be *a society that finds its greatness in the courage of protecting both its humanity and its economy as a whole.*

I concur with all the obstacles and building blocks given by the Global Icons.

In order to overcome these obstacles and to deliver the building blocks, the following kairos events are prerequisites to develop the kind of society that can build and sustain a WOIG-kind future:

(1) To build and sustain a modern, robust well-functioning economy that delivers broad-based economic prosperity and security.

(2) To cultivate a societal culture of giving, tolerance, and being respectful, without compromising on its values and aspirations to a WOIG-kind future, thus an active civil society having the wisdom, love, and courage to make hard choices.

(3) To cultivate a societal love for reading and learning from the classics (such as history, literature, art, music, philosophy, and anthropology) in order to develop a 'global stewardship mindset' as the only true and sustained alternative to an all-pervasive destructive mindset of bellicosity, greed, and other dysfunctional behaviours.

(4) To develop the following business leadership attributes: social intelligence, emotional intelligence, cultural intelligence, ecological intelligence, geographical intelligence, and religious intelligence.

(5) To restore societal trust in business leaders. For this, new relationships that are dear to society need to be developed

as a whole to deliver positive intergenerational results. For this business' responsibility . . .

> towards itself is to be an organ of society;
>
> towards its direct stakeholders is to be sustainable;
>
> towards the earth is its alignment with the earth's finite nature;
>
> towards the global commons is to be a co-custodian thereof;
>
> towards society is to be a co-architect of a healthy society;
>
> towards democracy is to protect its own operating space;
>
> towards government is its alignment with government priorities; and
>
> towards transnational crime is to eliminate its role and influence.

Socrates: What kind of business will such kind of society require?

Global leader

My *vision* is of a business that is world class, measured in terms of its role in the local and regional economy, whether it applies global best practice—for example, a rigorous and systematic approach, delivering industry-leading results over the business cycle; its transparency; whether it's globally connected; whether all its planning and actions are aimed at sustainable growth; whether it deploys capital profitably for shareholders, while all stakeholders are well-informed about, and educated in, the firm's vision and mission; and lastly, whether it plays its part in global challenges.

The key *value* would be that of acting as a value-adding organ of society, driven by a strategy implementation culture without compromising on integrity. Delivering this kind of value-proposition would require from business: to build a prosperous society and a harmonious world as an end-purpose of its vision; to be compliant with all relevant local and global responsibility indices, such as the Global Compact and the Kyoto Protocol; and lastly, to compassionately and creatively straddle the human pyramid with its goods and services.

The key *obstacles* in the turn-around to building such a world class business would be a lack of understanding the drivers of change arising from the external business, societal and political environments, and a lack of understanding of how to apply prudent responses thereto, that is, understanding and dealing with context.

Regarding the *building blocks*, I am convinced that we need to deliver real growth through research and innovation, requiring high levels of analytic decision-making skills and creativity; through collaborative strategies, requiring partnerships with all stakeholders; and, through strategy implementation and operational excellence.

Nobel laureate

My *vision* is of a business that can translate visions of social upliftment into sustained actions.

The key *value* would be the alignment of day-to-day business practice with basic religious values as the foundations of society.

The religious values I have in mind are the Judaeo-Christian commandments: 'thou shalt not steal or covet thy neighbour's possessions'—the basis of market property rights; and, 'thou shalt not commit murder or adultery or bear false testimony'—the basis of a cohesive society.

The key *obstacle* in the turn-around to building such a kind of business would be a lack of sound judgement in decision-making.

In addition to overcoming the above obstacle, the key *building block* in the turn-around to this delightful kind of business is the redefinition of 'entrepreneurship' to include the dual motive of making a profit and doing good. This would create sustained economic empowerment to the 3 billion people at the bottom of the human pyramid by way of leveraging on the empowerment of women, creatively and massively rolling out technology, infostructure, and education for the benefit of the poor, applying intergenerational economic principles, and lastly, aligning business strategies with government's and the UN's Millennium Development Goals.

Author

Reflecting on the Global Icons' dialogue, I conclude that it is not surprising to note that the global leader had a much clearer view of what kind of business a society needs. Not surprisingly either, it was the Nobel laureate who provided the deeper philosophical underpinnings for the global leader's views. Superficially though, these two views appear to be in conflict, and they sometimes play out as a conflict between business and society.

When such conflict happens at, for example, the annual civic protests surrounding the World Economic Forum's meeting, it is mostly due to a mutual incomprehension of the context surrounding the same issues. Business leaders and social activists argue for the same vision, but from the perspective of different realities pertaining to implementation type questions, namely: What . . . ? When . . . ? Where . . . ? How . . . ? Who . . . ? How . . . ? What resources . . . ? What trade-offs . . . ?

Issues that struck me from the Global Icons' dialogue are:

> The Nobel laureate's value statement that societal and business values should be aligned. The question is, which values come first? Before answering this question, I am reminded that the end-state vision for a WOIG-kind society is 'to find its greatness in the courage to protect its humanity and its economy [businesses] as a whole'. Therefore, there is no conflict in society's dictating the kind of business values it desires—after all, business is an organ of society, and not the other way around! This is also analogous to John Locke's Social Contract, where societal values dictate political conduct.

> I am concerned that the same term may have different meanings, for example, 'a world-class business' may have different meanings in world orders of destructive globalisation and of inclusive globalisation. This calls for a new language for a new world.

> I am also concerned that business is getting unduly burdened with all the many indices that it has to comply with in order to demonstrate responsible behaviour.

> I was pleasantly surprised to learn of business' new role to provide 'solutions without borders' to counter 'threats without borders', the reason being business leaders operating comfortably across country borders, which is in contrast to

political leaders who are stuck within their country's borders. Societal leaders, who are mostly local operators, focus on local problems while the origin of these problems may be in a different part of the world. Such a new working relationship between business, society, and government will require unusual working relationships, and will no doubt open new business opportunities.

The turn-around to a business as an organ of a WOIG society is likely to be an evolutionary process, while the firm needs to remain financially robust and competitive. Therefore, new risks will have to be taken incrementally to give management and shareholders time to adjust to the value propositions in a WOIG.

I was surprised to learn that the Global Icons state that integrity is a prerequisite for strategy implementation excellence—I thought it was a given!

Many of the proposals for a WOIG-kind business resonate with Edith Penrose's *Theory of the Growth of the Firm*[7], which was based on a sample of American firms which have been in business for more than 50 years since 1959. This theory identified four drivers of sustained business success, termed entrepreneurial services namely, versatility, ingenuity, ambition, and judgement. Unknowingly, and to my surprise, the Global Icons re-confirmed, re-contextualised, and expanded the original theory to include eight drivers of sustained business success in a WOIG-setting. These eight drivers (entrepreneurial services) are now entrepreneurial versatility, trust-building ingenuity, entrepreneurial ambition, entrepreneurial judgement, entrepreneurial innovation, entrepreneurial implementation, intrapreneurial operations, and entrepreneurial stewardship.

Given the above, my transformative redefinition of the kind of business a WOIG society needs is *a world-class business—financially robust across economic cycles, with global stewardship as the dominant business logic*.

I concur with all the obstacles and building blocks given by the Global Icons.

In order to set systemic drivers of change in motion, the following *kairos* events are prerequisites to build a WOIG-kind of business:

(1) To cultivate a business culture that understands that a stable societal environment is a prerequisite for sustained profitability, that is, that the firm is not the whole, but a part of the whole.

(2) To cultivate a business culture of winning through the creative application of multidisciplinary knowledge, global learning, and learning from history, that is, to seek competitive advantage outside the narrow confines of the firm's niche.

(3) To develop a corporate decision-making process that considers the holistic context of issues, and to assess it from different perspectives and from different modes of thought before coming to any conclusion, that is, to use both linear and holistic thinking.

(4) To develop an enterprise-wide dual capability to manage in both a local and a global environment, in both a high and a low technology environment, in both a first and a developing world environment, and at both the top and bottom ends of the human pyramid.

(5) To develop an enterprise-wide capability to deliver on the key drivers of sustained business success, namely:

Entrepreneurial versatility: moving beyond management and technical competence to build a WOIG enterprise as an organ of a WOIG society;

Trust-building ingenuity: convincing a sceptical audience about the merits of the enterprise's intent to turn around to a WOIG, and then to invest therein;

Entrepreneurial ambition: moving away from the comfort zone of destructive globalisation towards building a new WOIG-kind future;

Entrepreneurial judgement: having the ability to make holistic decisions through analysis and wisdom to advance the cause of good for all stakeholders;

Entrepreneurial innovation: having the ability to innovate in technologies, education, mindsets, and value-propositions necessary for a turn-around to a WOIG;

Entrepreneurial implementation: having the ability to master the art, science, and craft of implementation without compromising on quality, time, budget, and integrity;

Intrapreneurial operations: having the ability to exploit technologies and opportunities to optimize the firm's assets towards delivering sustained prosperity to a WOIG society; and

Entrepreneurial stewardship: having the wisdom, love, and courage to exert path-breaking leadership to apply the Social Contract with Business as an intergenerational business case.

Socrates: What kind of a leader would such kind of business require?

Global leader

My *vision* is of a business leader who can envision the future, and then lead to it. Such a business leader would be an entrepreneurial pioneer, able to work with political and societal leaders to enhance human prosperity and social justice. He or she would be a balanced person with a global mindset, and hungry to lead in a path-breaking manner.

The key leadership *value* would be 'championship of the light'. This implies that he or she must have a remarkable ability to refrain from the abuse of power; have courage; have conviction; have physical, emotional, and intellectual strength; have perseverance; be reconciliatory; and be responsive to social injustice.

These values drive the business leader's primary task, namely, to be a long-term wealth builder for which he or she must be able to balance conflicting interests and/or priorities; be able to deal with resistance to change; be resourceful, patient, disciplined, empathetic, and professional; and have a sense of good entrepreneurial timing.

The key *obstacle* would be the difficulty of learning to understand and to deal with changes in context.

Regarding the *building blocks*, I would focus on the following: the ability to expand intellectual thought beyond the current limits of leadership education; the ability and wisdom to become a long-term wealth builder; the ability to sell a vision or a purpose to diverse stakeholders; the ability to cultivate an entrepreneurial and/or an intrapreneurial culture; and to develop the ability to make holistic multiple-choice decisions with positive intergenerational results for stakeholders.

Nobel laureate

My *vision* is of a business leader whose decisions advance the cause of good—making choices that advance the well-being of humankind.

The key *values* for such a business leader are vested in the 'values of the light', namely, courage, integrity, endurance, self-discipline, and sustained commitment to carry out his or her beliefs in God; being universalist, tolerant, realistic, and true to inner convictions; respecting his or her spouse, minorities in society and future generations; pursue a dream that is bigger than self; a stewardship mindset; and having a conscience.

The key *obstacles* in the turn-around to develop such kind of business leader would be: not understanding what drives choices; not reading beyond the narrow confines of his or her professional speciality; not having an understanding of, and an empathy for, the poor; and not having courage to 'be the first drop' towards delivering a WOIG.

In addition to overcoming the above obstacles, the following *building blocks* are critical: to develop a business leader's ability to make flexible complex long-term decisions; and the ability to manage the innovation process over time—even across the time span of his or her time in office.

Author

I was struck by the overwhelming tone of spirituality and pioneering nature as a WOIG-kind business leader, when listening to the Global Icons. In this regard, I would like to comment as follows:

The core values of a WOIG-kind business leader have been described in very specific and broad-ranging characteristics that fit into the spiritual term of 'being a beacon of the light'. This openly spiritual tone is in stark contrast to the belief that business values are secular and amoral. However, this spiritual tone is in line with the path-breaking work of the prestigious Academy of Management's special interest group, 'Management Spirituality and Religion'.

It's also interesting that the Global Icons envisage the WOIG-kind leader not merely to be an entrepreneur, but that he or she should be a 'path-breaking' kind of entrepreneur, that is, through the entrepreneurial spirit to open radical new ways of doing business.

The Global Icons specifically highlight the following business leadership competences: to be able to access their higher faculties of thinking, conscience, and calling; to think in global and intergenerational terms; to be able to exercise judgement to advance the cause of the WOIG; to draw on their inner strength to act in ways that rise above themselves and their own term in office; to be able to envisage the oncoming world (i.e., to apply *kosoryoku*); and implementation excellence through integrity.

The words used by the Global Icons to describe the WOIG-kind leader resonate with wisdom (holistic, higher mode thinking), love (spirituality, conscience, and responsibility), and courage (to be a path-breaker for the light). To apply this language in practice would require a new vocabulary and new educational paradigm to develop such WOIG-kind business leaders. This new tone of language is not tolerated by mainline business, yet it's comes directly from today's most powerful global leaders and thinkers. Why this anomaly?

Given the above, my transformative redefinition of a WOIG-kind business leader is: *a business leader with the ability to envision the WOIG, and then to lead thereto in an entrepreneurial and path-breaking manner exerting leadership qualities associated with the Golden Rule of Humanity.*

In order to set path-breaking systemic changes in motion, the requisite *kairos* events are:

(1) to cultivate a global mindset, oriented towards a WOIG-kind future;

(2) to develop the ability to make holistic decisions that advances the cause of a WOIG;

(3) to cultivate a personal ethic of responsibility towards a WOIG-kind future; and

(4) to develop an educational paradigm that is aimed at educating a specific kind of leader for a specific kind of future, that is, a WOIG-kind leader for a WOIG-kind future.

In conclusion

The above Socratic dialogue definitively answers the question: change, yes, but to what?

Humanity gave its business leaders the mandate to deliver:

> *a WOIG, where systemic poverty has been permanently removed and where humanity's broad security is assured; requiring . . .*

a society that finds its greatness in the courage of protecting both its humanity and its economy as a whole; requiring . . .

a world-class business—financially robust across economic cycles, with global stewardship as the dominant business logic; requiring . . .

a business leader with the ability to envision the WOIG, and then to lead thereto in an entrepreneurial and path-breaking manner exerting leadership qualities associated with the Golden Rule of Humanity.

The elegant simplicity and the awesome implications of humanity's global sustainable mandate are indeed breathtaking . . . and . . . it's just as breathtaking to realise that the delivery of this mandate is the new reality for business leadership!

Thankfully, from the Socratic dialogue also emerged an avalanche of implementation guidelines: from identifying key obstacles and specific programmes to overcome these obstacles to path-breaking *kairos* events required to set systemic changes in motion.

However, as a seasoned global business executive, I want to do one more validation of this research-based mandate before proceeding to the application part of this book.

Therefore, in the next chapter I subject this mandate to the brutal scrutiny of business leaders-in-practice as a reality check.

1   Nain, M. 2006. *Illicit: How Smugglers, Traffickers, and Copycats are Hijacking the Global Economy.* Privately published through Eric Olsen Publishers, USA.

2   *Time*, 24 March 2008—Quoting UN research figures on global population growth.

3   Global Trends 2025: www.dni.gov/nic/NIC_2025_project.html.

4   Recited by Gunnar Berge (Chairman of the Norwegian Nobel Committee), in praise of Kim Dae-jung during the Presentation Speech, www.nobelprize.org.

5   Carroll, T. H. 1959. 'A foundation expresses its interest in higher education for business management', *The Journal of the Academy of Management*, 2(3): 155-165.

6   Kasser, T. 2002. *The High Price of Materialism.* Cambridge, MA: MIT Press.

7   Penrose, E. T. 1959. *The Theory of the Growth of the Firm.* Oxford: Basil Blackwell.

CHAPTER 5

A Brutal Reality Check

The objective of this chapter is to address any expressions of doubt about the merits of a turn-around to a WOIG, and also to provide a reality check on humanity's global sustainability mandate to its leaders.

In order to do this, I shared my research outcomes with my MBL Class of 2009 during lectures in Johannesburg and Addis Ababa. From some 500 highly critical post-graduate students (all full-time business leaders-in-practice from across all sectors of industry), emerged the following typical expressions of doubt, namely:

(1) 'A WOIG?—it's unrealistic, and an idealised world scenario!'
(2) 'The WOIG asks for a new approach to business, but business needs to make a profit!'
(3) 'What evidence is there that people want to change to a WOIG?'
(4) 'How can a WOIG be based on the wisdom of a Global Icon that I do not respect?'
(5) 'Why worry about turning to a WOIG—what will be, will be!'

Before proceeding, let us remember that doubt is a double edged sword. On the one hand, doubt is a powerful tool to resist change by either discrediting an individual, or by discrediting an argument. On the other hand, doubt as a method of inquiry is a wonderful way to discover and know for sure whether you are faced with a truth or a fallacy.

Regarding the first statement of doubt

'A WOIG?—it's unrealistic, and an idealised world scenario!'

Other expressions of doubt that fall into this theme are:

> ➤ 'Why did you select *Global Trends 2015* as the basis for global scenario planning?'
> ➤ 'It's unrealistic to assume that there would be no competition in a WOIG! Even Plato's Utopia did not work out!'
> ➤ 'It's a century problem—the turn-around to a WOIG should be tackled over a 100-year time span, maybe even a 1,000 years . . . [ha ha ha]!'

Why Global Trends 2015?

There are many futurists and long-term planning think tanks. I have decided not to use their work because it's either sensation-driven or it focuses on a specific niche, such as being country specific or industry specific.

I selected *Global Tends 2015* as framework for strategic thinking and debate because (a) its timing was appropriate—in 1999, at the turn of the twenty-first century; (b) its analysis was done in a scientific manner, and in consultation with non-governmental experts; (c) the assumptions were transparent; (d) it gave the global perspective of the national security policymaker of the USA—the world's leading economy, and global champion for freedom and democracy; (e) the scenario planning was done holistically and leadership language was used in the report; and, (f) it provides for a flexible and open-ended framework for further debate.

Why a world of inclusive globalisation?

For four good reasons: (a) it is the most favourable of all four probable global scenarios; (b) it is a best-fit with the voices from around the world (Chapter 1); (c) it is a best-fit with all global responsibility protocols, such as the UN's Global Compact; (d) it is a best-fit with all current technological and business model innovations to develop a sustained green economy; and, (e) it gives a very specific, unambiguous, and practical meaning to the end-game of global sustainability.

How long would the turn-around to a WOIG take?

I don't know, but I do know from history that humanity will not wait for another 100 years to bear the grotesque injustices it is facing. There is much evidence that the evolutionary turn-around to a WOIG has already started in many industry sectors, and in many countries. However, while the pursuit of a WOIG will remain a work-in-progress, every bit of progress is a step closer to the ideal end-state.

In this regard, let's take two examples from formerly closed economies to give proof that this quest is real and is happening right now. Global Icon Mikhail D. Prokhorov (Chairman of the Board of Polyus Gold, Russia), said, ' . . . we became the first Russian gold mining company which disclosed information about its business with such a degree of transparency'. Global Icon Jiang Jiaqing (Chairman of the Industrial and Commercial Bank of China), said, ' . . . in the new year, we shall devote ourselves to perfecting corporate governance in six aspects, namely . . .'. While these two company-specific initiatives are path-breaking, just imagine the many consequent virtuous spin-offs (i.e., the domino, or knock-on positive effects) to their clients and suppliers of goods and services.

Is a WOIG unrealistic?

Well, ask yourself the following questions from humanity's global sustainability mandate and then judge for yourself whether a WOIG is unrealistic or not, mindful of the wisdom from Descartes, 'I think, therefore I am':

What kind of future . . . ?

> . . . *to eliminate systemic poverty* . . . : Extreme poverty is not a human destiny. Is there anything wrong with creating the world's largest new market of some 3 billion people currently living on less than US$2 per day?

> . . . *to secure humanity's broad security* . . . : Extreme fear is not a human destiny. Anything wrong with today's global quest for environmental-friendly business practices?

What kind of society . . . ?

> . . . *to protect both its humanity and its economy as a whole* . . . : Can a society afford to protect only one of these two criteria?

What kind of business . . . ?

> . . . *a world-class business* . . . : Is this unrealistic?

. . . financially robust across the economic cycle . . . ? Is this unrealistic?

. . . global stewardship as the dominant business logic.: This is what a business as an organ of society would do. Today's corporate governance, corporate social, and environmental responsibilities are positive steps towards this criterion.

What kind of business leader . . . ?

. . . the ability to envision the WOIG . . . : A business leader who cannot envision should resign. Is it unrealistic to aspire to a better world for your children?

. . . in an entrepreneurial and path-breaking manner . . . : The entrepreneurial and pioneering spirit is a proven success driver towards prosperity. Is this unrealistic?

. . . while exerting the leadership qualities associated with the Golden Rule of Humanity . . . : The dark arts (e.g., bribery, extortion, trafficking, and deceit) are ways to success in a WODG. The Global Icons stated overwhelmingly that we need to turn away from these dark values. Is it unrealistic to aspire to get away from the dark?

You will agree that while delivering the WOIG is a tough challenge; it's not unrealistic but achievable, given time and responsible leadership.

Is a WOIG idealistic?

Of course, it's idealistic!

The WOIG is a best-fit of what humanity is aspiring to, and the most desirable of the four probable world scenarios. It aspires to a kind of end-game for global sustainability strategies, heeding the call of the voices from Chapter 1. It is a fusion of Western, Eastern, and Southern values and aspirations—and, it is aligned with your own inner dream to make this world a better place for future generations.

The question is whether it is achievable. For some it's a modern version of Plato's Utopia—good, but not achievable. For others it provides a blue-print to turn around from today's WODG. The pursuit of the UN's Millennium Development Goals by its 193 members is a good start towards a WOIG, and proof that the turn-around to a WOIG is considered a tough, but realistic ambition.

Any competition in a WOIG?

It would be a fallacy to assume that there would be no competitive forces in a WOIG. I envisage that the scramble for market share in the new WOIG economy will be as fierce as the scramble for resources, market share, and technology were in history—a scramble for first mover advantage.

Just think of all the innovative bottom-of-the-pyramid business models to capture small, but lucrative parts of the world's biggest emerging market of 3 billion people currently living on less that US$2 per day. It's just that the nature of competition will be different as is already evident in blue ocean strategies[1]—that is, making the competition irrelevant by way of opening up uncontested new (WOIG) markets. And, that business success will be measured differently, that is, the quest for optimisation rather than maximisation, the quest for stakeholder value rather than shareholder value, and the quest for sustainability rather than short-term success.

Conclusion

Aspiring to the WOIG is for thought leaders who have made a personal decision that it is a realistic and worthwhile ambition to pursue. These thought leaders will be inspired by the business scientist Gary Hamel who said that for the first time in history, companies can work backwards from their aspiration and imagination rather than forwards from their history.[2]

Global Icon Harish Manwani (Chairman of Hindustan Lever, India)

'Consumer relevant innovations, brilliant activation and outstanding execution were key drivers for our growth . . .

Project Shakti now has over 30,000 women entrepreneurs (Shakti ammas) selling our products in 100,000 villages in 15 states. This is providing empowerment and a much needed income opportunity to rural women folk and simultaneously increasing the penetration of your company's products where there is no developed retail network. Project Shakti demonstrates what can be achieved at the point where social responsibility, sustainability and business strategy all meet.'

Regarding the second statement of doubt

'The WOIG asks for a new approach to business, but business needs to make a profit.'

Other expressions of doubt that fall into this theme are:

> ➤ 'Business is not a charity—it needs to survive the competition.'
> ➤ 'Milton Friedman said that "the social responsibility of business is to make a profit". Why then all this other stuff to think about? He also said that the business of business is business'.
> ➤ 'Is there is a limit to a firm doing well?'
> ➤ 'Do you propose that social entrepreneurship should replace for-profit entrepreneurship?'

Should business make a profit?

Certainly, business needs to make a profit!

Profit is the entrepreneur's reward for having survived the competition and the economic cycle and for having managed to break even after inflation, tax, debt, and cost of capital.

This applies to both the WODG and the WOIG, but with different mindsets at work. Let me explain this by way of an analogy: a beast lives to eat—likewise, in a WODG, a firm exists to make a profit; a human eats to live—likewise, in a WOIG, a firm exists to make a difference.

The business philosopher, Charles Handy, gave intellectual depth to this analogy by asking, 'What's a business for?' He concluded that a business, as an organ of society, needs to make a difference to all its stakeholders. To do this, he introduced the concept of 'delightful organisations',[3] that is, businesses that go beyond the profit motive to also play a meaningful role in society. He cited various examples of firms doing just this across the world, such as the Global Icon Muhammad Yunus (Chairman of the Grameen Bank in Bangladesh) who earned the 2006 Nobel Price for Peace 'for his efforts to create economic prosperity from below'.

It is a grotesque fallacy to expect business to go bankrupt in order to make a difference to society. Going bankrupt is not in the interest of any stakeholder. The leadership challenge is to find a prudent way of delivering optimal sustained prosperity to all its stakeholders.

Is business a charity?

No!

Neither is business a legitimate entity for thieves, gangsters, white collar criminals, and other suchlike immoral operators from the underworld.

Is the social responsibility of a firm to make profit?

This was the wisdom of Milton Friedman[4] (Nobel Laureate for Economics, 1976). Today, we know that it was a fallacy. St. Augustine (345-430) cautioned against the same fallacy when he said that it is the greatest of all sins to mistake the means for the end.[5] The economist John Maynard Keynes[6] (1883-1946), also exposed this fallacy when he said that capitalism is the mistaken belief that the wickedest of men will do the wickedest of things for the greatest good of everyone.

Both Keynes and St. Augustine cautioned against the pursuit of profit without any notion of responsibility.

Is there a limit to a firm doing well?

The flip side of this question is: Is there a limit to a firm doing badly?

Both questions lead to a fallacy, namely that 'doing good business' and 'doing bad' are synonymous—alternatively said that 'being bad' is a prerequisite for 'good business'. Sadly, this fallacy is one of the anchors in today's business education, and the MBA qualification in particular. Sumantra Ghoshal[7], an esteemed business science professor, exposed this fallacy in 2005 when he critiqued business schools failing themselves and society due to a sixty-year legacy of amoral management education and developing management theories void of any moral responsibility.

In a WODG, the 'being good' is done by the Chairman's Fund or the Social Responsibility Department, while the rest of the firm continues 'doing bad' (i.e., 'doing good business')—an acute case of corporate schizophrenia!

Alternatively, in a WOIG, the entire business model revolves around 'doing good'—delivering directly or indirectly on each criterion of humanity's global sustainability mandate. The reality is that this is already happening. Just ask yourself which of the following two kinds of press releases you read mostly:

> . . . of a business leader who is intent on destructive behaviour, so as to increase the output of greenhouse gasses; or

> . . . of a business leader who is intent on constructive behaviour, so as to reduce the output of greenhouse gasses.

Will social entrepreneurship replace for-profit entrepreneurship?

Let's begin by distinguishing between the two types of entrepreneurs as per the Skoll Foundation[8]:

'Entrepreneurs are essential drivers of innovation and progress. In the business world, they act as engines of growth, harnessing opportunity and innovation to fuel economic advancement. Social entrepreneurs act similarly, tapping inspiration and creativity, and courage and fortitude, to seize opportunities that challenge and forever change established, but fundamentally inequitable, systems.

Distinct from a business entrepreneur who sees value in the creation of new markets, the social entrepreneur aims for value in the form of transformational change that will benefit disadvantaged communities and, ultimately, society at large'.

No, I do not see social entrepreneurship replacing for-profit entrepreneurship. It is not a case of 'either . . . or', but rather of 'and . . . and'. Both have a unique and complementary role in society. I envisage social entrepreneurship playing a bigger and more integrated role in the mosaic of organs of society in a WOIG.

From the Socratic dialogue, we have learned about the importance of entrepreneurial services for delivering sustained prosperity. In addition to these drivers of long-term sustainability, I propose that entrepreneurship should become the glue that binds a WOIG society's mosaic of organs together into one economic delivery system as a whole.

I believe that the more diverse these organs of society are, the more robust a WOIG economy would become. The diversity of these organs of society covers the broad spectrum from for-profit entrepreneurship, to social entrepreneurship, to environmental entrepreneurship, to global commons entrepreneurship, to NGO entrepreneurship, to governmental intrapreneurship, and to employees' intrapreneurship. All working separately, but co-operatively and collectively, towards delivering a robust WOIG economy, stimulate creativity and competition to the benefit of the WOIG consumer.

Conclusion

A WOIG society certainly requires a new approach to doing business. A WOIG business may be seen as the next natural step on the evolutionary curve towards a *holos* society. The current position on this evolutionary curve is today's quest for corporate social and environmental responsibility.

Certainly, up scaling on the evolutionary curve towards a WOIG-way of doing business will require new value propositions, new customer behaviour, and new investment criteria—all calling for responsible leaders to deliver path-breaking acts of wisdom, acts of love, and acts of courage.

Global Icon Rex Tillerson (Chairman and CEO of ExxonMobil, USA)

'. . . are testament to the strength of our long-standing business model—a rigorous and systematic approach, which delivers industry-leading results over the business cycle.

. . . reducing emissions from our facilities; deploying energy-efficient technologies across our global operations; working with partners to improve our customers' fuel efficiency; and investing in research to foster development of global energy technologies with significantly reduced greenhouse gas emissions'.

Regarding the third statement of doubt

'What evidence is there that people want to change to a WOIG?'

Other expressions of doubt that fall into this theme are:

> ➢ 'How can you expect the poor to aspire to the noble ideals of a WOIG?—they simply need food in their bellies!'
> ➢ 'Do you really think that people involved in organised crime want to become law-abiding, tax-paying, environmentally and socially responsible citizens?'
> ➢ 'Do you really think that businessmen want to be environmentally friendly and socially responsible?'

What evidence is there that people want to change to a WOIG?

How many examples of evidence do you need?

Let us begin with hundreds of millions of pieces of evidence! On 27 March 2011, that was the estimated number of people from 5,000 towns and cities across 134 countries who signed up for Earth Hour to switch off electricity for one hour to pledge their individual effort to counter global warming.[9]

Formal public domain reporting on sustainability, social responsibility, and compliance with corporate governance and responsibility indices are all part of today's normal business practice. Just Google any listed company, and you will be amazed at what is already being done! To get you started, have a look at www.ge.com where you will be introduced to General Electric's corporate culture of 'ecomagination', embraced by its 323,000 employees from around the world to drive growth by finding innovative solutions to environmental challenges.[10]

MBA graduates, traditionally known as *homo economicus*[11] (a rational self-interest maximiser), are undergoing a mindset change—today, research indicates that 97 per cent of Asian MBA graduates are willing to sacrifice financial rewards to rather work for a firm that is considered ethically and socially responsible.[12] The same mindset change would apply to MBA graduates from the West and South. It is reasonable to assume that, once these graduates become the captains of industry, the evolution to a WOIG will accelerate.

Should poor people pursue noble ideals rather than food to fill their bellies?

I pray that you will never be hungry, cold, sick, and without hope.

Poor people are 'bonsai people'[13], who simply need to be given access to an opportunity to grow out of poverty. Whilst survival from day-to-day is important, people's yearning for dignity, hope, and opportunity are more important in the long term. History taught us that poor people reach a point where dignity and hope is more important than daily food.

Will organised crime pursue the ideals of a WOIG?

No!

They will certainly be a formidable dragon to slay en-route to a WOIG. But it is no reason to surrender and to continue along the path of destruction, just because it is the easy option not to face the dragon. Already, it is a disgrace how many business, societal, and political leaders collude directly and indirectly with operators from the dark—just read your daily newspaper for evidence!

Will businessmen voluntarily be environmentally and socially responsible?

It is about where you are on the evolution curve from a barbaric society to a holistic society!

No wonder our Global Icons call for 'path-breaking leaders of the light' to lead the turnaround to a WOIG! Let us look at the precise words from our Global Icons describing the characteristics of the WOIG leader:

> From global leaders: *To become a champion of the light*
>
> To personify courage, conviction, strength . . . a lodestar of the light towards which we are working . . . to provide hope in turbulent times . . . to feel your pain [to recognise the voice of ordinary people] . . . the critical act of reconciliation . . . a remarkable ability to refrain from corruption, abuse of power, and the pursuit of good governance . . . to respond voluntarily to create a better society . . . being thoughtful . . . a sense of responsibility . . . a genuine respect for others . . .
>
> From the Nobel laureates: *To have leadership qualities of the light*
>
> Leadership qualities are courage, integrity, and sustained commitment to carry out your belief in God . . . to acknowledge the role of your spouse as a pillar of strength, a confidante, and inspiration . . . to have endurance, self-discipline, self-belief, true to inner convictions . . . to show reverence to the unknowable

[being intelligently ignorant] . . . universalist, tolerant, and rationalist ideals . . . to strive for a moral legitimacy by taking part in societal quests for fairness . . .

In a WODG, business leaders will certainly not want to act responsibly. At best, they will comply with responsibility indices through a game of bluff and deceit to portray an image of respectability. However, in a WOIG, business is seen as an organ of society that wants to act responsibly to all stakeholders.

Those businesses that do not want to act environmentally and socially responsible will eventually lose their social licence to operate. Global gatekeeper organisations, global civil society, and the global capital market will force them otherwise—watch this space!

Conclusion

There is much evidence that people want to turn away from today's WODG to a WOIG. The real question is: how do you respond to the voices calling for . . . yearning for change?

Global Icon Jeffrey Immelt
(Chairman and CEO of General Electric, USA)

'To be a reliable growth company requires an ability to conceptualise the future . . .

Our ecomagination™ initiative is designed to drive growth by creating innovative solutions to environmental challenges. We have already launched 45 products and have engaged hundreds of customers. When we started, we had $6 billion of revenues in ecomagination products; in 2006, we had $12 billion; and by 2010, we are targeting more than $20 billion.'

[As a consequence of the above, 2,537 patent applications were filed by General Electric in 2009]

Regarding the fourth statement of doubt

'How can a WOIG be based on the wisdom of a Global Icon that I do not respect?'

Other expressions of doubt that fall into this theme are:

> ➤ 'I do not like Thabo Mbeki—he was an XXX'; I do not like Boris Yeltzin, he was a YYY'; or 'I do not like Jiang Zemin—he was a ZZZ'.
> ➤ 'How do I know that you have not been biased in the selection of the Global Icons?'
> ➤ 'Your sample of business leaders is loaded with oil and gas barons—I am uneasy about them controlling the global agenda for change'.

Can all Global Icons be respected?

Well, I also do not like some of the global leaders that were selected!

Nobody is perfect—even Global Icons, despite their high office, have weaknesses.

But whether a global leader is deemed a hero or a villain, the reality is that, for a period of time, these people had the power and the means to change the course of history. For instance, under Thabo Mbeki's watch, he did ensure that the free market became the economic delivery mode for South Africans, rather than the nationalisation that his political party demanded; Boris Yeltzin stepped in at the critical moment to ensure that Russia continued its path of reform (remember his impromptu fiery speech on top of a military tank in Red Square to swing the mood of angry people towards positive change?); and Jiang Zemin led the Communist Part of China towards accepting modern economic reforms, which brought enormous prosperity to millions of Chinese.

Wasn't your selection of the Global Icons biased?

As you will recall from Chapter 3, I originally designed the sample selection criteria in order to get a balanced spread of global leaders and thinkers. For this, I had to comply with fifty-three academic research criteria in my doctoral research to prove trustworthiness. Hence, be assured that I had no control over the actual personalities selected for the sample of Global Icons (see Appendix B).

You could say that I have selected the 'chair', but not the individual sitting in the 'chair'!

Isn't there an undue influence by oil and gas barons?

Again, their selection was purely a function of the sample selection criteria. Their dominance in the global economy is a reality, and is reflected as such in the sample of Global Icons. My research confirms that they have a dual role of extreme importance to play. On the one hand, they improve the efficiency of carbon-based energy to protect their vested interests. On the other hand, they have the management and the resources to also develop the next wave of the world's green energy supply by way of extremely high-cost, high-risk research.

I envisage that the twenty-first century will be dominated by a scramble for new energy sources as oil and coal supplies diminish. It is conceivable that today's 'dirty-energy barons" will re-invent themselves to become 'green-energy barons' in order to maintain their market share in the extremely lucrative global energy market. Thus, their dominance in the global economy will continue to be a reality for a very long time. Deal with it!

Conclusion

Whether you do or don't respect a particular global leader, it does not matter. The reality is that the mix of global leaders shaping a new world will always consist of villains and heroes. The real question is whether you, in your own sphere of influence, are blocking the villains of the dark and supporting the heroes of the light?

**Global Icon Lázaro de Mello Brandã
(Chairman of the Board of Bradesco, Brazil)**

'. . . it is either grow or grow! . . . with realistic and consistent goals . . .

. . . the celebration of fifty years of Fundação Bradesco. A pioneer action of social investment, it is the greatest effort within the private initiative, and, certainly, one of the world's largest ones. The Foundation, with 40 Schools distributed all over Brazil, provides free and quality education to more than 108,000 students'.

Regarding the fifth statement of doubt

'Why worry about turning to a WOIG—what will be, will be!'

Other expressions of doubt that fall into this theme are:

> - 'God holds His creation in His hand—it may look bad now, but God will not let things go out of control.'
> - 'From history, I know that He has always intervened after a period of hardship.'
> - 'What can I really do? I am just a powerless individual in a big world. I may die anytime. So I might as well indulge myself and be happy!'

Why worry? God will fix it all, anyway.

It's a religious fallacy to reason that man is free to act as he or she pleases—acting carelessly or irresponsibly is not a religious virtue.

Whilst religion teaches that God holds His creation in His hand, mankind has been given a stewardship role in it. This calls for mankind to act responsibly as guardian of the earth.

On a practical note, the Stern Report's finding[14] in 2006 that human activity contributes to today's global warming and ecological degradation is research-based evidence that mankind is failing its stewardship calling. This reality of stewardship failure has been accepted by all responsible global leaders, religious or not. This acceptance of stewardship failure is today driving the planetary pursuit of sustainable development.

Global stewardship is the pinnacle of responsible human endeavour in life and in work. It is the new frontier of responsible leadership, and it is also the new frontier of competitive advantage in a WOIG economy.

What can I really do?

Being helpless is not a human destiny!

Read, reflect, and be inspired by the many voices cited so far in this book. You, as an individual, can start a revolution—beginning with yourself!

I can hear you say 'But how?'

You have heard about the 'delightful organisation'. Well, why not begin by being a 'delightful person' by being mindful over the one thing that you have absolute control over, namely, the kind of language you use as a business leader . . . ?

> **Tolstoy**
> 'Everyone thinks of changing the world, but no one
> thinks of changing himself.'

This concludes the research phase of the book answering the question 'change, yes, but to what?' A definitive research-based answer had been given, and all reasonable expressions of doubt have been dealt with in a sincere manner. We will now turn our attention to articulating a passage from research to application, drawing on the outcomes of the Socratic dialogue.

In the next chapter, I will introduce a new language for WOIG business leaders.

---

[1]   Kim, W. C. and Mauborgne, R. 2005. *Blue Ocean Strategy—How to Create Uncontested Market Space and Make the Competition Irrelevant.* Boston: Harvard Business Press.

[2]   Hamel, G. 2000. *Leading the Revolution.* Boston: Harvard University Press.

[3]   Handy, H. 2002. What's business for?, *Harvard Business Review,* 80(12): 49-55.

[4]   Friedman, M. *The New York Times Magazine,* 13 September 1970.

[5]   Werther Jr., B. and Chandler, D. 2010. *Strategic Corporate Social Responsibility: Stakeholders in a Global Environment.* Thousand Oaks: Sage Publications.

[6]   www.quotes.net/quote/14785.

7 Ghoshal, S. 2005. 'Bad management theories are destroying good management practices', *Academy of Management Learning and Education*, 4(1): 75-91.

8 www.skollfoundation.org.

9 www.earthhour.org.

10 http://en.wikipedia.org/wiki/General_Electric.

11 Ghoshal, S. 2005. 'Bad management theories are destroying good management practices', *Academy of Management Learning and Education*, 4(1): 75-91.

12 Montgomery, D. B. 2005. 'Asian management education: Some twenty-first century issues', *Journal of Public Policy and Marketing*, 24(1): 150-154.

13 From Muhammad Yunus (Nobel Laureate for Peace, 2006). He used this term to make a plea for poor people to be given access to opportunity and the means thereto, saying 'Poor people are not "bonsai people", society just needs to give them space to grow', www.nobelprize.org.

14 *Stern Review: The Economics of Global Change*. 30 October 2006 <http://www.hm-treasury.gov.uk/independent_reviews/stern_review_economics_climate_change/stern_review_Report.cfm.

Note: All references to chairmen—see Appendix B.

PART 3

THE SOCIAL CONTRACT WITH BUSINESS

What is Stewardship?

Stewardship is a philosophy—*Dalai Lama*

Today, more than ever before, life must be characterised by a sense of universal responsibility, not only nation to nation and human to human, but also human to other forms of life.

Stewardship is a religion—*Genesis 2: 15*

The Lord God took the man and put him in the Garden of Eden to work it and to take care of it.

Stewardship is an act of love—*St. Augustine*

Love, when it's true, is always directed away from yourself as a service to others. Service is love in its dynamic form— to work for others and the common good.

CHAPTER 6

A NEW LANGUAGE FOR BUSINESS LEADERS

The sociologist, C. Wright Mills[1], said that it is a flaw of humanity not to comprehend the historical context of its time. Likewise, it is a flaw of today's business leaders not to comprehend humanity's global sustainability mandate, unless a new language is used. Such a new language will empower you to understand its embedded values and relationships, the meaning of each success criterion, and to search for new ways to enrich your own business leadership acumen in order to deliver this mandate.

Such a new language will certainly draw upon your higher faculties of thinking, conscience, and responsibility to deliver a WOIG future—*requiring* a WOIG society, *requiring* a WOIG business, and *requiring* a WOIG business leader.

The intellectual journey towards discovering this new language begins by unpacking the deeper understanding of each word used to describe the WOIG business leader, namely:

> ***global leaders with the ability to envision the WOIG, and then to lead thereto in an entrepreneurial and path-breaking manner exerting leadership qualities associated with the Golden Rule of Humanity.***

Let's now begin with the word, *Global* . . .

Global implies a flexible leadership competence across the full spectrum of the human pyramid, and across the full spectrum of technology and geographical location—such kind of leadership competence calls for *wisdom*.

. . . leaders . . .

This word applies to all people with the *courage* to make a difference, whether it's a person with a formal leadership title or a person acting as a leader in his or her own community.

. . . with the ability to envision the WOIG . . .

This calls for *wisdom* to understand the reality of today's world's destructive ways, and that a WOIG offers a viable alternative.

. . . and then to lead thereto . . .

This calls for acts of *wisdom* to identify the key obstacles to be removed, and the key building blocks to be put in place for the turnaround to a WOIG.

. . . in an entrepreneurial . . .

To *courageously* and innovatively set in motion all forms of entrepreneurial energy as the key driver of the turnaround to a WOIG.

. . . and path-breaking manner . . .

This calls for acts of *courage* to become the 'first drop' that sets the forces of turnaround to a WOIG in motion.

. . . exerting leadership qualities . . .

This calls for *love* to act decisively as a different kind of leader—a leader of the light, a beacon of hope, and an inspiration to humanity as stated explicitly by the Global Icons.

. . . associated with the Golden Rule of Humanity.

This calls for leadership acts of *love* to reach out to make a real and sustained difference, which is the common denominator of all responsible leaders' finest achievements in history—and, will also apply today and into the future as a timeless quality of true leadership.

In conclusion, WOIG leadership stands on the pillars of wisdom, love, and courage.

For applied wisdom, the business leader would ask 'What is the truth in this situation?' Once this has been established, the next logical question would be 'What act of love will advance the truth in this situation?' Thereafter, the leadership question would be focused on the courage needed to implement, namely, 'What is the optimal way to implement this act of love to advance the truth in this situation?'

Let's now look at a number of practical examples from around the world where the above logic has been applied—and, the incredible impact thereof on the two key variables driving a WOIG, namely, to increase humanity's broad security along the X-axis, and to eliminate systemic poverty along the Y-axis as depicted in Figures 2.1 and 4.1.

Wisdom

What kind of wisdom would give birth to *a WOIG where systemic poverty has been permanently removed and where humanity's broad security is assured*?

Are there examples of this kind of wisdom being applied that could inspire and guide you to make a contribution to the turnaround to a WOIG?

—Yes. Let's look at the following examples of applied wisdom:

In 1860, the Royal Bafokeng tribe[2] in South Africa lost its land due to political forces at the time. Over the next 150 years, the 'People of the Dew' have worked tirelessly to restore their dignity, self-sufficiency, and hope. Today, they are the most prosperous tribe in Africa. Their Bafokeng Holdings have assets of some US$10 billion under management, making it the world's largest community-based investment company.

Muhammad Yunus[3] asked what would happen if the power of the free market could be harnessed to solve the problems of poverty and inequality? To find the answer to this question, lead him on a journey starting with his resignation as an economist in the USA to become the founding Chairman of the Grameen Bank in Bangladesh. Through innovative micro-finance business models he empowered the poorest of the poor to become micro entrepreneurs. This earned him the Nobel Prize for Peace in 2006.

On 30 October 2006, the Stern review 'economics for global change'[4] was issued, exposing the fallacy that human activity does not contribute to global warming and ecological degradation.

This report was since accepted by all responsible global leaders, resulting in today's quest for global sustainability. Today, US-dollar billions are spent around the world to develop new technologies, business models, and mindsets to apply global stewardship in all spheres of human endeavour.

On 18 April 2011, Rick Fedrizi[5], CEO of the United States of America's Green Building Council who has, since 2002, certified more than 1,000 energy saving projects in existing buildings around the world, said, 'The work itself is not cutting-edge, but it's about doing the basics better—but the savings add up: some 200 million metric tons of carbon would no longer be emitted each year'. The Empire State Building in New York slashed its utility bills by US$4.4 million per year which is one such example of applied wisdom to rather do the basics right than embarking on high cost demolitions and erecting new buildings.

Love

What kind of love would give birth to *the kind of society that finds its greatness in protecting both its humanity and its economy as a whole?*

Are there examples of that kind of love being applied that could inspire and guide you to make a contribution to the turnaround to a WOIG?

—Yes. Let's look at the following examples of applied love:

Mahatma Gandhi once said, 'No culture can live if it attempts to be exclusive'. Pranab Mukherjee[6] (India's Finance Minister) was mindful of this when he delivered his budget speech on 28 February 2011, encouraging India's bankers to reach out to an additional 73,000 unbanked villages. Financial inclusion aims to eliminate poverty from the excluded parts of society through personal empowerment.

Professor Mervin King[7] championed the corporate governance movement in South Africa. The King Report on Corporate Governance is widely used today as a global best practice benchmark for corporate governance. This is an act of love that protects the broad security of millions of stakeholders, including pensioners, widows, and vulnerable workers and their families. It also protects and guides company directors towards responsible business leadership, giving them a sense of purpose and meaning in their endeavours.

The Fair Trade[8] movement aims to assist vulnerable producers of goods and services in developing countries with markets in the developed world. The overall principle is fairness and equity between buyers and sellers. Fair Trade certified sales for 2008 which was worth US$5 billion from some 7.5 million producers and their families from around the world, who would not have otherwise had the ability to enter the global market. This achievement is in line with the Fair Trade Foundation's vision of 'a world in which justice and sustainable development are at the heart of trade structures and practices so that everyone, through their work, can maintain a decent and dignified livelihood and develop their full potential'.

As a young boy, Allan Gray[9] was struck by the unfairness that his cricket playmates did not have the same educational opportunities as he had. He decided to do something about it. This motivated him to build his own investment firm, Allan Gray Limited. As an act of love, it annually contributes 5 per cent of pre-tax profits to South Africa's largest private bursary scheme, aimed at students from disadvantaged communities. They also provide an extensive emotional and life-skills support service to their bursars.

Courage

What kind of courage would give birth to *world-class enterprises—financially robust across economic cycles, with global stewardship as the dominant business logic?*

Are there examples of this kind of courage being applied that could inspire and guide you to make a contribution to the turnaround to a WOIG?

—Yes. Let's look at the following examples of applied courage:

During the 1950s, nearly the entire fishing village of Minamata[10] in Japan was wiped out by mercury contained in the industrial waste water of the Chisso Corporation's chemical plant. This lethal cocktail poisoned the villagers' drinking and fishing waters that caused neurological diseases, disfigurement, and death. Due to the collective courage from thought leaders in the community, business, and government, Minamata recovered from this industrial tragedy by rehabilitating its land, its fishing waters, and its people. Today, the town of Minamata is a world leader in the treatment of consumer waste through innovative business models.

In May 2010, the Norwegian Ambassador[11] sent a note of protest to the South African Government about its Director General of the

Department of Labour, who was promoting personal business under the guise of official bilateral discussions. This protest was done in the public domain, and at the risk of fouling a valuable bilateral relationship between the two countries.

The development of the world's first US$100 computer[12] is about making profit, and giving 'bonsai people' (the world's three billion poor people) access to information, knowledge, and opportunity in order to help themselves. This initiative spurred on similar initiatives[13] such as the One Laptop per Child Association and the One Laptop per Child Foundation—an example of Benjamin Franklin's saying of 'doing well by doing good'.[14]

The Gencor Board[15] had to approve a US$1 billion investment to expand its aluminium smelter in South Africa. All investment criteria were positive. However, the key uncertainty was political instability as apartheid was entering its final stages during the early 1990s. As chairman Derick Keys and his board members came back from lunch in a down-town restaurant, they were drawn into a violent political demonstration in the streets. Later, when back in the boardroom, and thankful that nobody got hurt, a unanimous decision was taken to approve the investment, the deciding factor being that as responsible business leaders they needed to provide hope and confidence in the new South Africa.

In conclusion, the above reasoning and examples from practice dispel the myths that wisdom is for philosophers only, that love is for lovers only, and that courage is for dead heroes only.

Just imagine the kind of language that the following Global Icons used in their planning, organising, leading, and control, which earned them a place of honour in history:

Jimmy Carter (Nobel Laureate for Peace, 2002): ' . . . *for his decades of untiring efforts to find peaceful solutions to international conflicts, to advance democracy and human rights, and to promote economic and social development'.*

Wangari Muta Maathai (Nobel Laureate for Peace, 2004): ' . . . *for her contribution to sustainable development, democracy, and peace [in Kenya and Africa]'.*

Lui Xiaobo (Nobel Laureate for Peace, 2010): ' . . . *for his long and non-violent struggle for fundamental human rights in China'.*

In the next chapter, I will introduce the Social Contract with Business as the means to deliver sustained sustainability through leadership acts of wisdom, love, and courage.

---

[1]   Mills, C. W. 1959. *The Sociological Imagination*. London: Oxford University Press.

[2]   www.bafokengholdings.com/.

[3]   Yunus, M. 2007. *Creating a World Without Poverty*. New York: Public Affairs.

[4]   www.hm-treasury.gov.uk/independent_reviews/stern_review-economics_climate_change.

[5]   *The Times*, 18 April 2011: Greening the Skyline, p. 44.

[6]   *Business India*, 3 April 2011: A Game Changer, p. 78.

[7]   www.mervynking.co.za/pages/cv.htm.

8   http://en.wikipedia.org/wiki/Fair_trade.

9   www.allangrayorbis.org.

10   http://en.wikipedia.org/wiki/Minamata_disease.

11   http://www.africascan.com/node/3687.

12   www.gizmag.com/go/4687/.

13   http://en.wikipedia.org/wiki/One_Laptop_per_Child.

14   Various   sources,   such   as: www.time.com/time/nation/article/0,8599,1921444,00.html.

15   Jones, J. D. F. 1995. *Through Fortress and Rock—The Story of Gencor 1895 to 1995*. South Africa: Jonathan Ball Publishers, and, as informally told to the author by one of the Gencor directors.

CHAPTER 7

THE SOCIAL CONTRACT WITH BUSINESS

Social contract theory development started with John Locke[1] in 1690 with his *Two Treatises of Government*, where he put two very significant concepts together into one philosophy—the theory of the radical individual and the theory of the negative state. This theory is considered the basis of today's democracy as a political ideology, where the government acts as a trustee of societal values and aspirations for a specified term, where after the society decides whether it wants to entrust the same political party as its trustee for another term by means of a free and fair election. In all democratic countries this is enshrined in their constitutions.

Whilst social contract theory development is ongoing[2], little progress is made to the advantage of business leaders. It is almost exclusively the research domain of sociology, philosophy, and ethics. The notion of a social contract with business remains vague, unwritten, and suspect of undermining the profit motive of the firm. The inexcusable reasons for this fallacy are discussed in Chapter 9 and 12, and Appendix A, but is best summarised by the management scholar, Sumantra Ghoshal, who said that business schools have failed society and themselves with a sixty-year research tradition that is void of any notion of conscience or moral responsibility.[3]

Thankfully, visionary leaders in business and business schools who have mastered the new language of wisdom, love, and courage are advancing positive initiatives in responsible leadership and corporate social responsibility. Consequently, there is increased acceptance that a stable business environment is a prerequisite for sustained business, and also, that for this, some kind of compact between business and society is required.

Whilst perfect stability of the business environment is not possible, the business leader's challenge is to anticipate change and then pro-actively and holistically smooth-out the impact thereof on the firm. This activity is a new frontier of the firm's competitive advantage—crafting a sustained stable business environment within which the firm can prosper as an organ of society. Delivering such a stable business environment has become a core leadership competence, but with little research-based guidance on how to deal with it in practice.

This book aims to break the tradition of silence about the social contract with business, and the fallacy that it may undermine the profit motive of the firm. From my research in business leadership, the Social Contract with Business emerged as a theoretical model in business science explaining the key relationships driving sustainability of the firm as depicted in Figure 7.1.

Figure 7.1 The Social Contract with Business—as a theoretical model

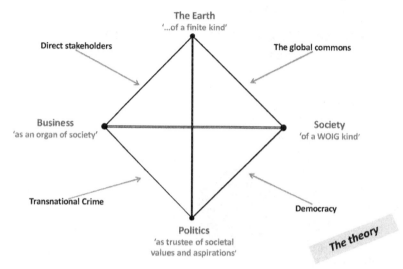

The Social Contract with Business
8 relationships that drive sustained sustainability

Source: Author.

Taking the above theoretical model to the level of applied business science, the eight relationships are redefined as eight leadership responsibilities as depicted in Figure 7.2. Whilst each leadership responsibility is important in its own right, it is incapable to deliver sustained sustainability on a stand-alone basis. All eight leadership responsibilities must be seen collectively as one whole.

As an analogy: A diamond's brilliance comes from a unique combination of four success criteria namely, carats, colour, clarity, and cut—that is, carats on its own is good, but does not contribute solely to the diamond's brilliance. Likewise, the Social Contract with Business' brilliance comes from a unique combination of all of its eight success criteria. For example, if a firm excels in all success criteria except to eliminate transnational crime, the firm's sustainability will remain an illusion. For robust and long-term sustainability (i.e., sustained sustainability) of the firm there can be no blind spots.

Figure 7.2 The Social Contract with Business—as a business case

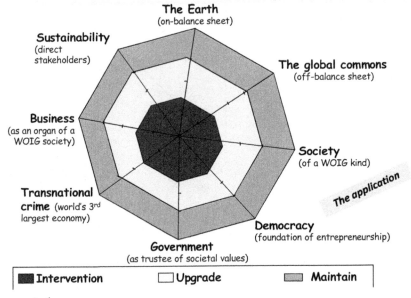

Source: Author.

Together these eight leadership responsibilities inspire and direct the business leader towards applying global stewardship as a business case to deliver sustainability for the firm.

The Social Contract with Business is neither another theory, nor another compliance checklist. In contrast, it is a practical business leadership tool defined as:

The Social Contract with Business is a business case that delivers sustained sustainability.

The business case consists of business' responsibility directed . . .

> *towards itself is to be an organ of society;*
> *towards its direct stakeholders is to be sustainable;*
> *towards the earth is its alignment with the earth's finite nature;*
> *towards the global commons is to be a co-custodian thereof;*
> *towards society is to be a co-architect of a healthy society;*
> *towards democracy is to protect its own operating space;*
> *towards government is its alignment with government priorities; and*
> *towards transnational crime is to eliminate its role and influence.*

Sustainability can only be achieved if humanity's global sustainability mandate is delivered, namely:

> *a WOIG, where systemic poverty has been permanently removed and where humanity's broad security is assured; requiring . . .*

> *a society that finds its greatness in the courage of protecting both its humanity and its economy as a whole; requiring . . .*

> *a world-class business—financially robust across economic cycles, with global stewardship as the dominant business logic; requiring . . .*

> *a business leader with the ability to envision the WOIG, and then to lead thereto in an entrepreneurial and path-breaking manner exerting leadership qualities associated with the Golden Rule of Humanity.*

In order to provide some contextual clarification to the above definition, it must be remembered that it is a model that makes global stewardship a practical reality; it is a lens through which to view the context of the firm in terms of leadership responsibilities; it is a holistic model that guides business leaders towards a higher ethic of responsibility for the future; it is part of a systemic whole of social contracts, mainly with society itself and government; it aims to restore and retain the trust of society in its business leaders; and, it adds value to ongoing theory development about the interface between business and society.

In the next section, each of the eight leadership responsibility domains will be introduced separately.

Business' responsibility towards itself is to be an organ of society

Such a virtuous responsibility can only be taken up if a firm reinvents itself to become a WOIG kind of business.

Achieving this would involve a cultural, ethical, and mindset change towards the values of a WOIG. Thereafter, it would require the creative application of all management tools and best practices to deliver on four priorities within a new WOIG market, namely, to survive a downturn in the economy, to break even financially, to provide a return on investment, and to deliver sustained prosperity to all stakeholders. This applies to all businesses irrespective of their size, the stage of their life cycle, or their industry sector. It also extends to all organisations within society and government, which are increasingly being managed along professional management and sound business principles to ensure efficient cost-effective delivery of goods and services to society.

The new reality is that society needs robust and competitive businesses as engines of long-term prosperity, that is, the ability to apply stewardship as the dominant business logic.

This new reality discounts the fallacies that attempt to undermine the powerful role of business as an organ of society, namely, that amoral (and, even immoral) business values are a prerequisite for success, that business is the whole of life, and that the only metric of success is profit.

Business' responsibility towards its direct stakeholders is to be sustainable

This responsibility is mainly achieved through compliance with socially and environmentally responsible indices and protocols, that is, to demonstrate compliance with external measures.

The objective is to protect the firm's reputation, to gain statutory permits to operate and to earn good investment rankings. The focus on integrated reporting on sustainable development has contributed much to begin the turnaround to a WOIG. A good example is the widely accepted 'triple bottom line' method of accounting, that is, reporting on financial, social, and environmental results, also known to the layman as the PPP (profit, people, planet) accounting method.

The new reality is to make sustainable development for all its stakeholders an integral part of the firm's business model. Alternatively said: to leave a legacy of positive influence within the business' sphere of influence.

This new reality counters the fallacy that compliance reporting is simply a game of bluff and deceit to keep share activists and social gatekeepers happy.

Business' responsibility towards the earth is its alignment with the earth's finite nature

This is done by way of *on-balance sheet* activities.

These are activities where both the firm and the earth benefit directly, such as carbon-neutral, water-neutral, or waste-neutral business practices. The earth's direct benefits are an increased ability to sustain life. The firm's direct benefits are that it becomes more competitive in a WOIG economy, attracts WOIG customers, investors, and employees, and its reputation soars with society and regulators—thus being considered as the preferred supplier of goods and services, as well as for any further new investment.

The new reality is that the earth has become the fourth party to the traditional tripartite global discourse between business, society, and government. The earth's voice is heard through its devastating impact on society when its life-supporting systems are disturbed. All responsible global leaders accept today that it is not only about human activities that pollute, but also about human activities like deforestation and reducing biodiversity, that take away nature's ability to heal itself.

The core fallacy that the earth's resources are infinite, which dominated political and economic thinking of the nineteenth and twentieth century, delivered today's WODG. This is a tragic chapter in the economic history of mankind—a testimony to the folly of man.

Business' responsibility towards the global commons is to be a co-custodian thereof

This responsibility is discharged by way of *off-balance sheet* activities.

The off-balance sheet activities comprise direct co-custodianship of the noosphere, biosphere, and the physiosphere. Co-custodianship implies maintenance, preventative, or rehabilitation activities. This is done in partnership with governments, NGOs, or societal organisations already active in commons issues, such as endangered wildlife, wetlands, and biodiversity. From these activities the commons benefit directly, while the firm benefits only indirectly.

The global commons also provides an immense new area of opportunity and growth for business. A good example is Wikipedia, which empowered millions of people by way of low-cost open source access to information and knowledge. Another example is that the rehabilitated commons offers immense opportunity for tourism, wellness, and recreation—which are all at the core of a healthy society.

Global Icons, Elinor Ostrom and Oliver E. Williamson (Nobel Laureates for Economics, 2009), placed the responsibility towards the commons firmly on the global economic agenda as a new reality. However, the slippery slope here is the general belief that the global commons belongs to nobody, yet is the responsibility of everybody. Sadly, the reality is that while everybody is concerned, nobody really takes responsibility for it.

To add to this sad reality is that very few people understand that the commons is actually the womb of all life on earth. It's not a human destiny to extinguish itself by its own irresponsibility—we are stewards of the miracle of life on earth. Thus, a new frontier for responsible business leadership and path-breaking entrepreneurship opens, which I term as 'global commons entrepreneurship', akin to social entrepreneurship.

Business' responsibility towards society is to be a co-architect of a healthy society

This is done through financial and non-financial social responsibility initiatives.

The old reality is for business to focus only on those societal needs which hold the promise of mass marketing impact, such as sport sponsorships.

The new reality is that business needs healthy societies in order to be healthy itself. For this, society needs to be empowered to help itself instead of only receiving financial handouts. Therefore, business needs to discover the wide variety of non-financial contributions, and the full spectrum of what constitutes a healthy society.

Non-financial contributions traditionally vary from making its facilities, technology, and know-how available to societal organisations, and to purchase goods and services from local suppliers. Just ask yourself: What creative applications of non-financial contributions to society lie beyond traditional thinking?

The richness of the drivers of a healthy society has been identified in the Socratic dialogue with Global Icons. Business can support society—

> to assert its classic, timeless values: the right to acquire property, the right to live one's life as one sees fit, and the right to liberty of conscience and opinion;

> to assert its modern values: the right to a society that is just (fair, equitable), harmonious (peaceful, stable and drug-free, with religious freedom, reduced inequality, and no discrimination on the basis of gender, race, religion, or heritage), secure (in terms of both basic human needs and physical security), and prosperous (moderately, sustainably);

> to assert its postmodern values: the right to a safe and clean living environment; access to information, knowledge, and opportunity (entrepreneurship, bandwidth); being protected from 'threats without borders'; and being able to appeal to the world in the case of political abuse; and

> to counter its negative societal inclinations, such as a culture of dependency on handouts, bellicosity, insatiable consumerism, self-serving, self-worshipping, exponential population explosion, a culture of silence about injustices, a culture of entitlement, racism, extremism, casteism, xenophobia, fundamentalism, alcohol and drug abuse, domestic violence, and collusion with transnational crime.

This new reality puts an end to the fallacy that a firm's social responsibility is to make profit, which was the Holy Grail for three generations (i.e., sixty years) of business leadership education (see Appendix A).

This new reality also calls upon society to play its part in the Social Contract with Business because any contract consists of at least two consenting parties.

Business' responsibility towards democracy is to protect its own operating space

This responsibility is aimed at gatekeeper institutions upholding democratic rule, which I term as 'corporate democracy responsibility', akin to corporate social responsibility.

Democratic rule protects business' operating space through the rule of law, security of tenure, property rights and so on. Yesterday's thinking is that the government will honour its social contract with society, thus business' operating space could be assumed a given.

The new reality is that most governments are shredding this social contract in many underhand ways to feed their own greed for power and money—the 1690 theory of the negative state is alive and well even today! Therefore, business needs strong democratic institutions in order to remain sustainable. Business has a dual responsibility here, namely, to support (or counter) government action, but also to support government and societal gatekeeper organisations. In fact, they become the invisible hand that protects the social contract between society and government.

In this regard, business needs to discover the mosaic of civil democracy gatekeepers such as institutes, forums, NGOs, social media outlets, and influential individual people. Whilst all of them are fiercely protective of their independence, they all need business and societal support to continue with their work to counter the negative state. Even governmental institutes that uphold democratic structures need the support of business and society. Unfortunately, abusive governments are notorious to weaken their own democratic structures and institutions in order to shred the social contract with ease.

The new reality is that business needs to protect its operating space with the same zeal as its own social and environmental responsibility initiatives.

Business' responsibility towards government is its alignment with government priorities

This responsibility aims to support government to deliver on its reasonable objectives.

Today, there is increasingly a political leadership vacuum and even political leadership paralysis. Whilst governments are stuck within a country's borders, business is not. Much of what happens today to a country's citizens originates outside the country's sovereign borders where politicians have no authority. This leads to the logic that 'threats without borders' need 'solutions without borders'. To add to this dilemma, today's emerging market governments have enormous developmental responsibilities which are typically beyond their ability to deliver in terms of scope, complexity, quality, and cost-efficiency.

The new reality is that the above political dilemma opens enormous growth opportunities for business to become a co-deliverer of government's objectives and to provide 'solutions without borders'. This may call for a variety of new business ventures either as sole co-deliverer, or in co-creating ventures with government departments or NGOs. As an organ of society business needs to address this political dilemma for the sake of its own sustainability.

This new reality of political co-responsibility and creatively establishing unusual alliances with non-business entities are new business leadership competences.

Business' responsibility towards transnational crime is to eliminate its role and influence

This responsibility needs to be taken-up with the same zeal as business has taken up its social and environmental responsibilities.

Transnational crime is arguably the world's third largest economy after the United States of America and the European Union. Its traditional unlawful activities are money laundering, smuggling, and trafficking of anything that makes profits by way of unlawful activity—from drugs to human body parts to arms to intellectual property. Other unlawful activities vary from white collar crime to institutional corruption.[4] Its influence in society and the economy is destructive in all ways imaginable.

The Global Icons' concern was that it is not only immoral criminals who are active here, but also ordinarily good people who have no restraint when an opportunity for easy money arises (with a low perceived probability of getting caught). Also, that organised business seems intertwined with, and even dependent on, global crime.

The new reality is that, while business' first line of responsibility is to eliminate internal crime, much more needs to be done to combat transnational crime. Unless this business leadership blind spot is addressed, sustainability will remain an illusion—a fool's paradise.

Business' responsibility towards the whole

Now that each of the responsibility domains has been examined independently, the focus shifts to the whole of the Social Contract with Business.

The Social Contract with Business can be applied on various levels, for example, for the corporation as such, per business unit, per department, per project, and even to assess an individual business leader's competency.

All eight global responsibility domains should be considered simultaneously and during all phases of the life cycle of the firm or the project. In practice, some responsibility domains will have a higher priority rating than others from time to time, depending on the ebb and flow of doing business. However, each responsibility domain needs to be assessed independently using either an analytical or a judgemental assessment technique. The scoring rules as given in Table 7.1 may be used for this.

Table 7.1 Scoring rules, associated risks and corrective plans

Score	Contribution	Risk	Type of corrective plans
2	Strongly positive	Low	Maintain
1	Good	Medium	Upgrade—slow, gradual steps
0	Neutral	High	Upgrade—fast, gradual steps
−1	Bad	Extremely high	Upgrade—quantum steps
−2	Strongly negative	Implosion assured	Intervention

Source: Author.

This assessment provides for the current reality to be profiled in the form of a spider diagram. Figure 7.3 provides an example of an ideal application of the Social Contract with Business—all eight leadership responsibilities are in the *'strongly positive; low risk; maintain'* assessment category.

Figure 7.3 The Social Contract with Business—an ideal profile

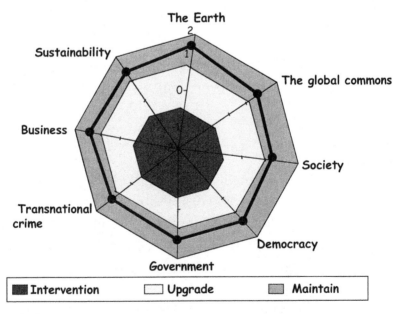

Source: Author.

In conclusion, for the business leader the Social Contract with Business provides . . .

➢ for a business case to deliver robust sustainability for the firm;
➢ for the delivery of humanity's global sustainability mandate;
➢ for a means to restore societal trust in business leadership;
➢ for the practical application of global stewardship;
➢ for a simple, yet powerful means to communicate complex issues to stakeholders;
➢ for allocating resources at the key areas that threatens the firm's sustainability;
➢ for a lens through which to view the context of a business in terms of action-oriented leadership responsibilities; and
➢ for discovering purpose and meaning in business leadership as a profession.

In the next chapter, I will introduce case studies from around the world in order to enhance your understanding of the Social Contract with Business, and also to put it in the context of your own reality.

---

[1]   Stumpf, E. S. and Abel, D. C. 2002. *Elements of philosophy: An introduction*, 4th ed. New York: McGraw Hill.

[2]   Various researchers, such as Conrey, E. J. 1995. A critique of social contracts with business. *Business Ethics Quarterly,* 5(2); Shankman, N. A. 1999. 'Reframing the debate between agency and stockholder theories of the firm', *Journal of Business Ethics,* 19: 319-334; Malachowski, A. 2001. *Business Ethics: Critical Perspectives on Business and Management.* London: Routledge; Donald, T. and

Dunfee, T. W. 1999. *Ties that Bind: A Social Contracts Approach to Business Ethics*. Harvard Business School Press.

3　Ghoshal, S. 2005. 'Bad management theories are destroying good management practices', *Academy of Management Learning and Education*, 4(1): 75-91.

4　Nain, M. 2006. *Illicit: How Smugglers, Traffickers, and Copycats are Hijacking the Global Economy*. Privately published through Eric Olsen Publishers, USA.

CHAPTER 8

CASE STUDIES FROM AROUND THE WORLD

The objective of this chapter is to deepen your understanding of the Social Contract with Business, and to integrate it with today's leadership discourse on more responsible ways of doing business.

The chapter begins with eight case studies, one for each of the eight leadership responsibilities embedded in the Social Contract with Business. These cases reflect some of my life's experiences as a global business executive working in 25 countries across 5 continents. The chapter ends with a case study that integrates all eight leadership responsibilities as a whole.

The case studies' setting:

> *SmartCo, a fictitious Australian-based multinational corporation (MNC), has sent three of its senior managers on a global tour to find new business ventures. They are John, Rajeshwari, and Karlheinz, representing SmartCo's North American, Indian, and European Union markets respectively. In-between their formal meetings they have an ongoing informal dialogue about the meaning of responsible business leadership.*

Reflection guidelines for the case study:

> *The critical questions asked; the perspective given; the facts given; the practical examples given; the subtle mindset shift*

*towards an ethic of responsibility to the WOIG future; and the
leadership action that follows reflection.*

Business' responsibility towards itself is to be an organ of society

One evening, over cocktails at the Raffles Hotel in Singapore,
Karlheinz laments about how hard it is to meet the criteria of a
WOIG enterprise. He concludes by saying, 'It's such a battle just to
survive the competition. It's difficult to focus on anything else, let
alone the pursuit of noble ideals.'

Rajeshwari said encouragingly, 'I agree that the global stewardship
requirement of a WOIG business is difficult. But at least, I understand
where all this effort to comply with social and environmental
responsibility indices fit into the big picture. For now, it seems to me
as if global stewardship as a business case is a work-in-progress.'

'The part about becoming a world-class business and being
financially robust across the economic cycle, is what we are trained
to do', said John. He continued, 'Take for example BHP Billiton who
mastered the first part of the definition. They are a fully diversified
global mining company, with all its business risks fully hedged.
BHP Billiton is considered a long-term blue chip investment and a
good global corporate citizen.'

John concluded, 'It seems like we have a dual responsibility. On the
one hand we have to build world-class businesses. On the other
hand, we have to play a midwife's role to deliver the world we all
want. This duality may cause us ultimately to end up even stronger.'

While looking at his cocktail, Karlheinz said reflectively, '*Dual responsibility*, you say . . . and, *ending up stronger* . . . this may then trigger a virtuous cycle: the stronger a firm gets, the more positive its influence in society, the more like-minded shareholders are attracted, the stronger the firm gets . . .' Later that evening, when back in his hotel room, he looked at www.bhpbilliton.com for global learning points from an industry leader to guide him in his further thinking about setting SmartCo's virtuous cycle in motion as a leadership act of courage.

Peter Drucker[1]

'Management has become the all-pervasive, the universal organ of modern society . . . For modern society has become a society of organisations. The overwhelming majority of all people in developed societies are members of an organisation; they derive their livelihood from the collective income of an organisation, see their opportunities within an organisation, and see their success primarily as opportunities within an organisation, and determine their social status largely within the ranks of an organisation . . . In a society of organisations, managing has become a social function and management the constitutive, the determining, the differential organ of society.'

Business' responsibility towards its direct stakeholders is to be sustainable

While still recovering from a cultural shock at last night's dinner in Yichang (宜昌市), in the Hubei Province of China, Rajeshwari asked, 'What does sustainability mean for a firm?—It is such a multilayered and multicultural concept!'

John, just back from a conference on sustainable development in France, said smugly, 'I like Ruben Gechev's definition: Sustainable development is socially justified and environmentally sound economic development.'[2]

'Well, that's good to get some clarity!' Karlheinz said. He continued, 'I guess that Standard Bank is doing sustainability right—they have survived and prospered for some 150 years. They survived two civil wars, being colonised, two world wars, the great depression of the 1930s, as well as epic socio-economic and political turmoil locally! Today, they are considered one of Africa's top banks, with a reputation to die for. Even their current CEO, Jaco Maree, is considered to be the most trusted CEO in South Africa, and is also included in the Financial Time's top 50 businessmen in emerging markets.'[3]

Karlheinz continued, 'At an International Conference on Responsible Leadership at the University of Pretoria in 2010, I remember him saying that some of the key issues that contribute to their sustained success are to stick to the basics of doing good business, to see opportunities where others see despair, to stay close to the customer and the society in which they operate, to manage their assets, mindful of their reputation and to find those partners [and clients] who also respect their values.'

Somewhat taken aback by such a simplistic business philosophy, Rajeshwari said, 'Well, I guess that those principles are loaded with unsaid wisdom and entrepreneurial acumen. I hope to find a lot more insight from www.standardbank.com to better understand their enduring practical wisdom.'

> **Global Icon José Sergio Gabrielli de Azevedo**
> **(President and CEO of Petrobas, Brazil)**
>
> ' . . . but Petrobas also won further important recognition of its
> performance: its selection for the Dow Jones Sustainability Index and the
> ISE (Bovespa Corporate Sustainability Index), and the classification of
> its shares as investment grade by the rating agency Standard and Poor's.
> These accomplishments all strengthen our faith that Petrobas is on the
> right path and will continue to grow profitably and show social and
> environmental responsibility.'

Business' responsibility towards the earth is its alignment with the earth's finite nature

Sitting in a taxi that's driving through the glitz and glamour of Ginza, the shopping district of Tokyo, John said, 'Can you imagine all the resources being mustered from around the world to fill all those shopping bags?' He continues, saying, 'I remember from the Socratic dialogue that the Nobel laureate said that 20 per cent of the world's population consumes 80 per cent of the world's resources. Should the remaining 80 per cent of the world also start consuming likewise, we would need four new Planet Earths real soon!'

Karlheinz said, 'Something needs to give. Either we need to consume less, or we need new business models, or we need new habits and mindsets—perhaps a combination of all.'

Rajeshwari, sitting next to Karlheinz, responded by saying, 'I remember that Tesco, UK's largest retailer, donated £5m to start the Sustainable Consumption Institute. They focus on the research areas of sustainable consumer behaviour and lifestyle, eco-innovation for sustainable production and distribution, and climate change and carbon mitigation. This is in line with the former CEO of Tesco, Sir Terry Leahy's vision to create new ways in which we live and work.'

Karlheinz, after listening carefully to Rajeshwari, said, 'That's good, but we also need business leaders to take a pioneering role to risk new business models, to risk intergenerational economics, to risk customer re-education, and to risk new economic delivery systems as an alternative to capitalism.'

Later that evening in his hotel room, John looked for reflection points from *www.sci.manchester.ac.uk* and *www.roundview.org* to guide him to reflect upon this new leadership challenge to create new ways for SmartCo's staff, customers, and shareholders in which to live and work. He was thrilled to find a new ambition that was bigger than himself and his board as an act of love towards future generations.

Global Icon Jorma Ollila (Chairman of Royal Dutch Shell, EU)

'The energy business, as I am seeing first-hand, is at the heart of some of the most important economic, environmental, and social issues facing the world. Reliable and affordable supplies of energy are essential for economic growth and for raising living standards amongst the world's poorest people. Equally, as the growing concern over climate change shows, providing those energy supplies in a way that minimises the impact on the environment is one of the greatest challenges we all face.

Shell is playing its part in addressing those challenges . . .'

Business' responsibility towards the global commons is to be a co-custodian thereof

While in a small airplane from Jakarta to Halmahera Island in Indonesia, Karlheinz looked down on vast areas of shark-invested sea and tropical forests. This made him remember a visit earlier that year to the Couga Mountains in South Africa. There he met a local community leader with a mile-wide smile! Within three years his tribe became prosperous—they now have running fountains, good grazing land, and a community chest of US$1m earned by clearing their ancestral land of alien plants that use high volumes of water.

Rajeshwari said, 'I remember that project. It is SABMiller that embarked on a mission to become a water-neutral firm—the first in South Africa!'

John told his colleagues that this project is called Water Futures, a partnership between SABMiller, WWF (World Wildlife Fund), and the Deutsche Gesellschaft für Technische Zusammenarbeit, acting on behalf of the Federal German Ministry of Economic Cooperation and Development. They intend to examine new ways to water management throughout SABMiller's value chain. This project is active in South Africa, Peru, Tanzania and the Ukraine. The project is proving that water stewardship can be a solid business case by offsetting excessive industrial water usage by way of restoring the water table in the commons.

Karlheinz listened carefully to their conversation, and decided to take SmartCo beyond being carbon-neutral to also become water-neutral, as a first in his country. And, if there can be a carbon exchange market to assist firms to become carbon-neutral, why not a similar water exchange market?

Later, when back in the Shangri—La Hotel in Jakarta, Karlheinz googled '*Water Futures Project, SABMiller*' for some global learning to guide his new ambition to become a business leader exerting path-breaking courage.

Global Icons Elinor Ostrom and Oliver E. Williamson
(Nobel Laureates for Economics, 2009)

'for her analysis of economic governance, especially the commons' and

'for his analysis of economic governance, especially at the boundaries of the firm' respectively.

Business' responsibility towards society is to be a co-architect of a healthy society

After three days of intense negotiations, it's time to relax at the pool of the Hotel Nacional de Cuba in Havana. Coming out of the pool, Rajeshwari asked, 'Do we really know what sustained good comes from social responsibility activities? Is it not throwing hard-earned money into a bottomless pit?'

Somewhat surprised, John replied, 'Well, there is certainly no end to sport sponsorships and making donations to charitable cases. I remember my first boss who said that help is defined by the recipient and not by the donor. With this wisdom he meant that we need to take time to find out what kind of help is required, and then to assist in a way that respects the dignity of the recipient. For him, such a bottom-up approach was the only way to achieve sustainable results.'

These comments triggered Karlheinz to remember an article he had to read for an Executive Development Course he did at a business school in Spain. He happened to have the article in his briefcase, and encouraged his colleagues to read the section he had in mind right away:

> 'One of the biggest societal concerns is the collapse of governmental services. To fill this need a new business model was developed, which was reported as follows: Finally, BP and the NGOs together have developed a business ecosystem that brings different economic entities—a global corporation, a local social organisation, informal micro-entrepreneurs, and a research institute—into an efficient value chain. This alliance offers the promise of more than just access to better products at more affordable prices; it gives people at the bottom of the pyramid, who until now were unable to enjoy the benefits of globalization, a chance to create new livelihoods and gain economic and social influence. The same pattern is visible in the cocreation partnerships between ABN AMRO and Accion; Telenor, Danone, and Grameen Bank; Microsoft and Pratham; ICICI Prudential and SEWA; Local Sustainability and CH2M Hill; Microcare and Aon.'

Slightly stunned, both Rajeshwari and John reached for their Blackberries to send a message to their secretaries to find the article: Brugmann, J. and Prahalad, C. K. 2007. Cocreating business's new social compact. *Harvard Business Review, February*: 80-90. Both agreed that it's a must-read! Also that if this can be implemented, it would certainly be a leadership act of love in each of the sixty countries in which SmartCo operates.

Jeb Brugmann and CK Prahalad[4]:

'The liberation of markets is forcing executives and social activists to work together. They are developing new business models that will transform organizations and the lives of poor people everywhere.'

Business' responsibility towards democracy is to protect its own operating space

While stuck in a traffic jam in New York opposite the United Nations' head office, John remarked highly irritated, 'These guys have great ideas about the world we want, but they do not know how to deliver.'

Karlheinz, also irritated about the delay, continued, 'It's a serious flaw! Can you imagine a world without democracy—a world where entrepreneurship, the free market, and the right to own property are outlawed? The pillars upon which our businesses are founded cannot be taken for granted!'

Rajeshwari, trying to calm her two companions, said, 'It's a cliché, but if ordinary people do nothing the worst will happen. A civil activist group, Avaaz (meaning 'voice' in some languages), is on a mission to close the gap between the world we have and the world most people want.'

Looking at *www.avaaz.org* (15 April 2010) on her Blackberry, she read the following to Peter and John:

'*The Economist* writes of Avaaz' power to "give world leaders a deafening wake-up call"; the *Indian Express* heralds "The biggest web campaigner across the world, rooting for crucial global issues", and *Suddeutsche Zeitung* calls Avaaz "a transnational community that is more democratic, and could be more effective than the United Nations". Avaaz empowers its members [13 million by February 2012, and growing exponentially!] to take action on pressing issues of international concern, from global poverty to the crises in the Middle East to climate change. Its model of internet organising allows thousands of individual efforts, however small, to be rapidly combined into a powerful collective force'.[5]

Both Karlheinz and John decided to become members of Avaaz and to spread the word. It is time that business leaders stand up to protect its own operating space, even only as members of social gatekeeper or activist groups. 'Political abuse needs to be countered on all fronts to protect business' operating space and the social contract', both agreed with the enlightened expression of new-found wisdom on their faces.

Ban Ki-moon[6]

'markets can flourish only in societies that are healthy, and societies need healthy markets to flourish.'

Business' responsibility towards government is its alignment with government priorities

While waiting in a board room for the next meeting, Karlheinz read from a local newspaper: 'Namibia has become the 22nd African country to invite AgriSA [the South African commercial farmer's union] to establish farms.'

'I am not surprised', said Rajeshwari. 'The best kept secret about South Africa is its 40,000 commercial farmers. Their experience comes from 360 years of farming profitably in the harsh African climate. Without receiving any subsidy from their government, they ensure that South Africa is the only African country (54 in total) that does not need to import food.'

John continues where Rajeshwari stopped, 'Sadly, they are in a love-hate relationship with their government, which hates them for not being politically loyal to them, and loves them for delivering food security. Despite this unfortunate relationship, these commercial farmers remain fiercely loyal to their country! This spurs them on to remain a force for positive change in South Africa, and Africa.

'Other African countries are openly luring South African farmers to assist them with building up their agricultural industries. So far, some 1,000 commercial farmers have entered the African agricultural market with unbelievable success. Ironically, the South African government hates them for taking their skills out of their country, but loves them for making their political dream of an economically strong Africa come true!'

'Just imagine, how quickly one billion Africans' dream of a prosperous Africa will happen if politicians support business leaders as their cross-border implementers of policies', said Karlheinz while looking for more information at *www.fin24.com/Economy/SA-farmers-offered-more-land-in-Africa-20100917*   to better understand being an agent of world benefit as a leadership act of profound love.

Thomas Maak[7]

' . . . corporations do indeed have a new political role in a connected
world, in particular with respect to human rights, social and
environmental justice . . . [thus] the emerging political co-responsibility
of MNCs.'

Business' responsibility towards transnational crime is to eliminate its role and influence

While travelling in the cable car up Sugar Loaf Mountain in Rio
de Janeiro in-between meetings, Rajeshwari asked, 'Is it true that
transnational crime is the world's third largest economy?

John, distracted from admiring the beautiful scenery, said, 'That's an
educated guess, because we simply do not know. For me the deeper
question is whether organised business should join government's
fight against organised crime?'

Karlheinz continued by saying, 'What organised business does is
to comply with anti-crime protocols, such as the Global Compact's
10th principle, which states that businesses should work against
corruption in all its forms, including extortion and bribery. Their
own ethical codes of conduct also emphasise integrity and honesty.
They are pre-occupied to counter their own internal fraud and
corruption. Whilst this is their first line of responsibility towards
clean business, organised business can play a much bigger role to
counter transnational crime. In particular, to counter disturbing new
trends, such as planned state failure.[8] Here, I think of Zimbabwe
where state failure was caused by rogue politicians in order to get

access to the country's wealth, and I also think of Pakistan where state failure was caused by terror groups to get access to nuclear weaponry. Then there is institutionalised crime like executive greed in organised business[9], and tenderpreneurship[10] by political party bosses doing business with their own governments.'

Karlheinz concluded the above perspective by asking reflectively, 'Why does it seem as if shredding the social contract and doing immoral kind of business are considered to be normal? Have we lost our souls so badly that we cannot distinguish anymore between right and wrong?'

Rajeshwari shook her head, and said, 'Something does not make sense—if global crime accounts for some 10 per cent of global GDP, then government and business are not doing what they claim to do. Or, is this their collective blind spot?' She then called her secretary to arrange a meeting with her local parliamentary representative to discuss ways in which she may contribute to the fight against organised crime, while wondering who will be the first business leader to receive the Nobel Prize for Peace . . . 'for his or her efforts to fight transnational crime in order to sustain the pursuit of sustainable business.'

Global Icon Azim H. Premji (Chairman of Wipro Technologies, India)

' . . . there was always this restless edge to do more, to achieve more . . . without diluting the focus on operational excellence that leads to flawless execution.'

These values guide us in all our transactions and relations. These values define what Wipro is and what we mean to our stakeholders. We call these values *Spirit of Wipro,* which manifests as an intensity to win, acting with sensitivity, and being unyielding on integrity all the time.'

Business' responsibility towards the whole

On a Quantas flight from London to Sydney, John was reading a book *The Social Contract with Business* by one Jopie Coetzee. He was captivated by the voices calling for change, the research-based mandate from humanity to deliver global sustainability, and the Social Contract with Business as a business case. He called on his travelling companions, who were bored to tears on this long-haul flight back to head office.

After explaining the Social Contract with Business to them, Rajeshwari said, 'Wow, this model puts all our loose conversations about a more responsible way of doing business in a coherent model, and provides for a powerful leadership tool to actually do it!'

Karlheinz said sceptically, 'Well, let's put this Social Contract with Business to the test by applying it to a real business case.'

Eagerly, Rajeshwari gave them the press release of 24 November 2010 from Business Report[11] which she had just finished reading:

'Unilever, which sells products in 170 countries, announced last week that by 2020 it would help: 1 billion people improve their hygiene habits and bring safe drinking water to 500 million people to reduce life threatening illness; reduce salts and fats from its foods; halve the greenhouse gas impact of its products across their life cycle; halve the water used on its products in water scarce countries; halve the waste disposal of it's products; source all its raw materials from sustainable sources; and improve the livelihood of 500,000 small scale farmers . . . but more innovation is needed.'

Together, they assessed this initiative based on the information available from the press release, and using the scoring rules from Table 7.1. John, Rajeshwari, and Karlheinz could not believe their eyes as Figure 8.1 unfolded, as their assessment progressed—it was so easy, so practical, and . . . so powerful!

The project seems well balanced across five of the eight areas of leadership responsibility, and that intervention will be required to improve its 'corporate democracy responsibility' and its role to eliminate transnational crime. The project's responsibility towards government also needs to be upgraded.

Immediately, Karlheinz, the well-known Doubting Thomas, said, 'Applying the Social Contract with Business is going to be *thé kairos* event for SmartCo.'

Both John and Rajeshwari responded by saying, 'Let's propose this to the Chairman of SmartCo during our feedback meeting tomorrow. In this way we can apply leadership acts of wisdom, love, and courage.'

Figure 8.1: The Social Contract with Business—an example

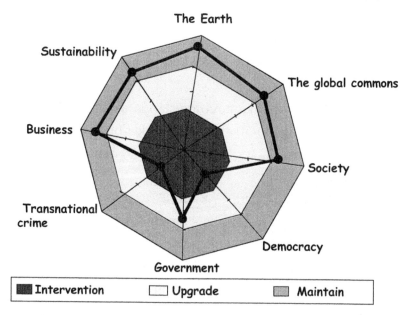

Source: Author.

In conclusion, personal buy-in to the Social Contract with Business is a function of accepting humanity's global sustainability mandate and the language of wisdom, love, and courage.

Some of you may ask, 'But if it's that simple, why is it not widely used already?'

This is a very good question. Therefore, in the next chapter I will introduce business leaders' blind spots that prohibit the application of the Social Contract with Business.

1   Drucker, P. F. 1987. 'Management: The problems of success', *Academy of Management Executive,* 1(1): 13-19.

2   Gechev, R. 2005. *Sustainable Development.* Indianapolis: Indianapolis University Press.

3   www.blog.standardbank.com/blog/standard-bank-team/2010/01/jacko-maree-among-top-50-emerging-market-business-leaders, plus the author's personal notes taken during Jaco Maree's speech at the University of Pretoria.

4   Brugmann, J. and Prahalad, C. K. 2007. 'Cocreating business's new social compact', *Harvard Business Review, February*: 80-90.

5   www.avaaz.org (15 April 2010)

6   On 24 September 2008, Ban Ki-moon (Secretary General of the United Nations) addressed leaders from business, government, and civil society at the first UN Private Sector Forum. www.un.org/News/Press/docs//2008/sgsm11815.doc.htm.

7   Maak, T. 2009. The cosmopolitical corporation. *Journal of Business Ethics,* 84: 361-371.

8   Chomsky, N. 2006. *Failed States—The Abuse of Power and the Assault on Democracy.* New York: Metropolitan Books.

9   Kothari, V. B. 2010. *Executive Greed: Examining Business Failures that Contributed to the Economic Crisis.* New York: Palgrave Macmillan.

10   http://multimedia.timeslive.co.za/videos/2010/01/tenderpreneurship-a-threat-to-good-governance-nzimande/.

11   www.iol.co.za:80/business/business-news/unilever-pushes-to-meet-targets-1.876094.

PART 4

APPLYING THE SOCIAL CONTRACT WITH BUSINESS

Pierre Teilhard de Chardin

Someday, after mastering the winds, the waves, the tides, and gravity, we shall harness for God the energies of love, and then, for the second time in the history of the world, humanity will have discovered fire.

CHAPTER 9

THE GLASS CEILING PROHIBITING APPLICATION

As you are now entering the application phase of this book, I assume that you are already well versed in strategy implementation. Hence, I will only focus on adding WOIG-kind value to your existing prowess as a business leader.

I begin this chapter by answering the question at the end of the previous chapter: if the Social Contract with Business is that simple, practical, and powerful, then why has it not been applied already?

Whilst it is true that some parts of the Social Contract with Business are already being applied through a myriad of corporate initiatives, the application of the whole thereof remains amiss. The reasons for this may be found in business leaders' **blind spots** which prohibit the application of the whole. These blind spots arise from forgotten old knowledge, that is, not knowing what you should know!

This is due to simple ignorance, or due to a dysfunctional educational system as exposed by the iconic business educator, Russel L. Ackoff[1], who said that business leaders are not stupid, but merely misinformed, incorrectly instructed, and do not understand the fundamental changes in their environments. Blind spots may also be due to knowledgeable business leaders who consciously choose to act irresponsibly, illegally, or unethically.

These blind spots are formidable barriers to change, which if not addressed, will keep the Social Contract with Business forever in the realm of theory development and suspect of undermining the profit motive of the firm. However, overcoming these blind spots will serve as unique entry points to break the glass ceiling that keeps you from applying the Social Contract with Business. Consequently, overcoming each blind spot is a personal business leadership challenge.

Let us now examine the key blind spots prohibiting the application of the Social Contract with Business.

Ignoring minor voices at your own peril

For a period of time soundless voices and societal voices can be ignored or even quashed, but over time they trump business voices. How many business enterprises today survived fifty years, or even ten years? Today, many business enterprises are adjusting their business models to counter their impact on global warming and ecological degradation in order to become responsible global corporate citizens—they have taken minor voices seriously.

Let's look at AVAAZ[2], a social media platform which makes minor voices count as evidenced in their press release of 8 November 2010:

'The global campaigning organisation Avaaz applauds Hilton Worldwide's commitment to sign a rigorous global code of conduct and create a network of Hilton employees in eighty-two countries and 3,600 hotels working against sex trafficking. Prompted by news reports of sexual exploitation in Hilton hotel rooms, over 300,000 Avaaz members from around the globe sent messages of concern to

Hilton's CEO, urging the hotel giant to immediately implement and enforce the Code of Conduct for the Protection of Children from Sexual Exploitation in Travel and Tourism'.

The consequence of this blind spot is that business leaders miss out on early-stage strategic signals pertaining to a change in the context of the business environment, which is the new frontier of competitive advantage.

The cowardly silencing of the inner voice

One's inner voice is mysteriously programmed to distinguish intuitively between right and wrong. Over time, this inner voice may be suppressed for a variety of reasons to deliver destructive business models. Today, amoral and even immoral firms are considered successful, and their business leaders are hailed as role models for young executives.

For example, can you name one business leader who is dedicated to finding sustained business models that are not dependant on insatiable consumerism? Do you remember the voice from Chapter 1, which said, ' . . . insatiable consumerism [fuelled by irresponsible marketing] was driving global warming and ecological degradation and destroying human values—a poison that corrodes what is good?'

Are you aware of the different kinds of moral fibres of a firm? They are as given below:

> The *immoral firm* actively opposes ethical and legal behaviour in business, and participates in both the underworld and the formal economy.

The *amoral firm* considers business and social values to be mutually exclusive. Business is unconcerned about ethics, but works to the letter of the law. For the sake of respectability it would comply with social and environmental codes of practice.

The *wavering firm* is uncertain whether business and ethics can be mixed. Their social and environmental compliances are exemplary, and they experiment cautiously with new business models and technologies that fit into a WOIG. However, when under some pressure it defaults back to amoral business practices.

The *moral firm* has embraced the Social Contract with Business. They fully capitalise on the opportunities offered by a WOIG. Their customers, employees, business leaders, and shareholders are all dedicated to high standards of ethical and responsible behaviour towards the future.

The consequence of this blind spot is a schizophrenic business leadership culture, that is, to be an admired economic hit man by day, and a concerned member of society by night.

The madness of aspiring downwards

Plato's 'Theory of Knowledge' introduces two modes of thought, namely, opinion and knowledge. The lower level of opinion-based thoughts consists of trial-and-error and experience, while the higher level of knowledge-based thoughts consists of science and philosophy. Thought leaders need to master all four modes of thought to ensure a rich and robust mix of decision-making tools. Yet it is tragic to observe how business leaders shy away from the higher modes of thought.

For example, business schools are under tremendous pressure from business to change their focus from education to skills training, and from critical thinking to finding quick-fix solutions to problems in case studies which are void of context and consequence.

The consequence of this blind spot is that leaders develop a shallow and short-term culture, which in turn then fuels the educational market for shallow business knowledge. It becomes a self-driven spiral towards lower and lower levels of knowledge, ethics, and responsibility—are the barbarians coming, or are they already here?

The daftness of negative belief perseverance

Whilst expressions of doubt are a positive method to pursue the validity of a truth claim, there is also a dark side to it. It is astounding to listen to business leaders who defend the WODG, despite the overwhelming evidence to the contrary. For example the mindless protection of a lucrative, but destructive business model due to pressure from shareholders or peers—or worst of all, cowardice due to a silenced inner voice. The consequence is that business leaders not only delay delivery of sustainability, but also attract a pathetic following of like-minded fools.

'*But* I am just doing my job to earn a living', says he.

The tragedy of reality confusion

Remaining in one's office and in front of a computer screen may easily lead to confusing artificial reality with real reality. The former makes it difficult to understand the hunger pains of the poor, the desperate flight of vulnerable ecological refugees, the humiliation of being uneducated, or the desperation of the unemployed. Understanding the impact of business models on human security is a new leadership challenge.

'*But* I cannot calculate fear, thirst, or disease into my financial spreadsheet—so it does not matter', says she.

Wisdom is for philosophers only

This blind spot denies business leaders' access to higher modes of thought. Reasoning based on the lower levels of thought are good, but need to be enriched with the language of wisdom to deal with today's complex world.

For example, wisdom helps the business leader to judge between short—and long-term priorities, local and global priorities, multiple stakeholder expectations, and decision-making in the absence of complete scientific data. Wisdom also helps to deal with ambiguity, conflicting priorities, conflicting expectations and demands, and the duality of leadership responsibilities. And, most importantly, wisdom clearly identifies the divides between fairness and unfairness, just and unjust, right and wrong, and the dark and the light; and then to craft a way forward towards delivering humanity's global sustainability mandate.

This blind spot begs the question 'What is the truth in each situation?' thus requiring a balanced application of all four modes of thought (i.e., trial-and-error, experience, science and philosophy) in decision making.

Love is for lovers only

Yes, love is not a word used in business. Yet it is what drives our quest for social and environmental responsibility. The word love is a verb with varying meanings—from the sensual to the hardest of hard decisions to deliver good as an end-state. Understanding and mastering the various types of love also serve as an intuitive guide to apply an ethic of responsibility to the future. A written corporate code of conduct is good, but need to be enriched by an intuitive application of love and to reach out.

For example, what will inspire and guide global leaders to pursue an alternative mode of economic delivery, such as eco-economic conservationism?

This blind spot begs the question: what act of love will advance the truth in each situation? This requires an understanding of the power of love as the invisible hand that guides responsible decision-making.

Courage is for dead heroes only

Yes, applying courage could be a deadly act! You may put your name and career on the line by taking a stand to defend a principle, or by taking some pioneering initiative.

For example, what will you do in your own firm when you hear the following contradicting statements from India, which is a water scarce country with a huge population?

— The CEO of a major cool drink manufacturing firm states that it only consumes 3 litres of fresh water to produce one litre of cool drink, that is, production-line thinking.

— An accredited water specialist states that it takes seventy two litres of fresh water to produce one litre of cool drink, that is, value chain thinking.

— A well-known professor asks, 'What's the point of India becoming an economic superpower, if it has to import all its fresh water from outside its borders?', that is, holistic thinking.

This blind spot begs the question: What is the optimal way to implement an act of love to advance the truth in this situation? What courage is required to address similar conflict of thinking in your firm? Thus requiring an inner conviction to stand up for the truth, no matter how small an issue may be at stake—a case of zero tolerance for half-truths and silence that covers up.

The foolishness of entrenched fallacies

This blind spot arises from a lack of critical thinking which was amply illustrated by some of the expressions of doubt in Chapter 5.

The consequence of this blind spot is that fallacies become entrenched as unquestionable business principles that cause incalculable, and even irreversible, harm over many years. Political strategists are well versed with the value of repeated fallacies.

The sadness of linear thinking in a holistic world

This bind spot keeps business leaders from understanding:

— that knowledge should not be compartmentalised;
— that a stable business environment is a pre-requisite for sustained business;

— that the Social Contract with Business is part of a systemic whole of social contracts, mainly between society and government, and between society and itself; and

— the powerful duality of humanity's global sustainability mandate, that is, to deliver a WOIG where poverty *and* human security is assured; *requiring* a society that finds its greatness in protecting its humanity *and* its economy; *requiring* world-class enterprises—financially robust across economic cycles *and* with global stewardship as the dominant business logic; *requiring* global leaders with an ability to envision the WOIG, *and* then to lead thereto in an entrepreneurial and path-breaking manner, *and* exerting leadership qualities associated with the Golden Rule of Humanity.

The consequence of this blind spot is resistance to change, because they simply cannot comprehend the elegant simplicity of holistic thinking, and the powerful and far reaching impact thereof.

The regret of missed small opportunities

This blind spot is about not being aware of opportunities that emerge unexpectedly wherever you may be or in whatever situation you may find yourself in (as was the case in each of the nine case studies from Chapter 8). A constant awareness to provide a little clarification, a little encouragement, or a little support goes a long way to inspire colleagues and subordinates, or even change the mindsets of executives and shareholders with significant positive results.

Let me give you an example: A while ago, a former MBA student approached me for a personal reference to include in his application for a doctoral study. Over a cup of coffee he said, 'All this talk and research about global warming are questionable. Since the beginning of time, nature self-healed after volcanic eruptions, released a zillion tons of carbon gasses into the atmosphere. I mean, what is the real significance of a small firm trying to reduce its carbon emissions?' My instinctive answer was, 'Remember, that nature's ability to self-heal has been severely compromised due to deforestation. Also remember that today there are a zillion small firms around the world whose collective impact on global warming may be equivalent to one volcanic eruption per annum.' A few days later he called to say that he changed his doctoral research topic to sustainable development.

It was a case of winning over a new champion for the WOIG—one by one! Just imagine the consequent incalculable positive spin-offs over the lifespan of this new champion of the WOIG!

The consequence of this blind spot is that thought leaders miss valuable opportunities to enlarge the pool of WOIG leaders by way of informal mentoring.

'What suggestions do you have to overcome all these blind spots?', I can hear you ask!

Yes, I do have a number of practical suggestions to overcome these blind spots.

To begin with, I do not wish that you become discouraged by all these blind spots, but rather to remove them enthusiastically because they have prohibited you to break the glass ceiling to enter the WOIG.

You also need to create awareness thereof for yourself and for the stakeholders in your business. A good start would be to make a poster (as in Table 9.1) of these blind spots that you can hang in your office, and at all locations where business decisions are taken.

Table 9.1 Blind spots prohibiting application of the Social Contract with Business

Blind spots to overcome
Ignoring minor voices at your own peril
The cowardly silencing of the inner voice
The madness of aspiring downwards
The daftness of negative belief perseverance
The tragedy of reality confusion
Wisdom is for philosophers only
Love is for lovers only
Courage is for dead heroes only
The sadness of linear thinking in a holistic world
The foolishness of entrenched fallacies
The regret of missed small opportunities

Source: Author.

You may also construct a large poster with a spider diagram displaying all the blind spots, with category indicators to suit your own reality, such as 'not overcome yet', 'being overcome' and 'overcame'.

Another technique may be to appoint a champion as a gatekeeper for each blind spot to actively ensure its absence in the planning, organising, leading, and control of the firm's endeavours. The appointment of such champions may become part of the career development the next generation of the firm's executive management.

In conclusion, you have been introduced to a wide range of blind spots that prohibit the application of the Social Contract with Business. Not all may apply to you, and you may even have become aware of a few personal blind spots—your own Achilles' heel.

In the next chapter, I will introduce a way to empower yourself as a WOIG leader who has freed himself or herself from the blind spots which have tied you down below the glass ceiling.

---

[1]   Allio, R. J. 2003. 'Russell L. Ackoff, iconoclastic management authority, advocates a 'systemic' approach to innovation', *Strategy and Leadership,* 31(3): 19-26.

[2]   https://secure.avaaz.org/act/media.php?press_id=219 (accessed April 2011)

CHAPTER 10

APPLICATION GUIDELINES FOR PERSONAL EMPOWERMENT

The objective of this chapter is to facilitate your personal growth to become a WOIG business leader.

In practical terms this means to sharpen your capabilities to apply the Social Contract with Business, whether you are a business, societal, or political leader, or simply an individual conducting your own affairs in a business-like manner.

This will be done by way of adding value to your existing business leadership acumen, which you may have obtained from one or more of the following educational modes:

> the University of Life, that is, learning from experience.
> formal education:

> > a master's degree in business administration (MBA).
> > a degree in politics, philosophy, and economics (PPE).
> > any other degree or executive development programme that covers the multidisciplinary nature of business leadership.

> simply by being a reader of quality business books, essays, newspapers, or magazines.

This journey of personal empowerment begins by reflecting on the scope of each of the building blocks and outcomes as given in Table 10.1. However, this will not be a passive kind of reflection. After reflecting on each building block, I expect you to identify your own educational gaps, and then to devise your own action plan on how to close the gap. For this, you may consider doing another course, self-study, or appoint a coach/mentor.

Thereafter, I encourage you to start applying your new WOIG capabilities in practice—starting off with a low risk application, and then gradually step up as you gain more experience and confidence.

Table 10.1 The growth-path of a WOIG business leader

BUILDING BLOCKS	OUTCOMES
Doing capabilities (leadership-in-practice capabilities)	Design, build, and maintain prosperity Global learning
Kairos capabilities (core capabilities)	Global mindset Holistic decision-making
Entrepreneurial services (to deliver a WOIG-kind enterprise)	8 leadership competences
Social Contract with Business (to deliver a WOIG)	8 leadership responsibilities
Language (a new vocabulary for a WOIG)	Wisdom, love, and courage
Turnaround strategy to a WOIG (to set in motion systemic success drivers of a WOIG)	18 *kairos* events
Kosoryoku (Western, Eastern, and Southern values and aspirations)	Humanity's global sustainability mandate (a WOIG)
Fundamental values (what makes humanity humane?)	The Golden Rule of Humanity

Source: Author.

Let us now reflect on each building block, its associated outcome, and the probable impact on your own personal empowerment.

Fundamental values

Yes, it's love and to reach out to others that drive today's corporate social responsibility and corporate environmental responsibility. And, it is also what knowingly or unknowingly drives your own quest for making a difference in life and work.

Yes, it's what gives purpose and meaning to the profession of a WOIG business leader.

Personal empowerment:

- ✓ Key learnings: . . .
- ✓ Action plan: . . .

Kosoryoku

Delivering humanity's global sustainability mandate is the raison d'être of WOIG business leadership. This mandate is the end-result (*kosoryoku*) of WOIG leaders' endeavours.

For the purpose of application, all strategies, projects, and operations in your organisation need to be assessed relative to their direct or indirect contribution to each criterion of this mandate, namely, to deliver:

— *a WOIG, where systemic poverty has been permanently removed and where humanity's broad security is assured; requiring . . .*

— *a society that finds its greatness in the courage of protecting both its humanity and its economy as a whole; requiring . . .*

— *a world-class business—financially robust across economic cycles, with global stewardship as the dominant business logic; requiring . . .*

— *a business leader with the ability to envision the WOIG, and then to lead thereto in an entrepreneurial and path-breaking manner exerting leadership qualities associated with the Golden Rule of Humanity.*

As a systems thinker, you will appreciate that the above four criteria are mutually dependent and mutually re-enforcing, that is, focusing on only one criterion will scuttle the whole of humanity's global sustainability mandate.

Personal empowerment:

✓ Key learnings: . . .
✓ Action plan: . . .

Turnaround strategy to a WOIG

What are the success drivers that will deliver a turnaround to a WOIG?

From the Socratic dialogue with the Global Icons, *kairos* events have been identified as the systemic drivers of humanity's global sustainability mandate. For application purposes, any turnaround strategy to a WOIG in your organisation needs to set in motion all the *kairos* events, namely:

What kind of future?

> To understand the current state of the world in terms of statistics and universal values;
> To have a personal ethic of responsibility towards the future (i.e., global stewardship);
> To understand the holistic and intergenerational consequences of business models on poverty and the broad security of society (i.e., conscience-based decision-making);
> Improved global communication about the state of the world, as well as the positive and negative trends thereof (i.e., a kind of a global dashboard).

What kind of society for such a future?

> To build and sustain a modern, robust, and well-functioning economy that delivers broad-based economic prosperity and security;
> To cultivate a societal culture of giving, tolerance, and being respectful, without compromising on its values and aspirations to a WOIG future. Thus, an active civil society having the wisdom, love, and courage to make hard choices;
> To cultivate a societal love for reading and learning from the classics (such as history, literature, art, music, philosophy, and anthropology) in order to develop a 'global stewardship mindset' as the only true and sustained alternative to an all-pervasive destructive mindset of bellicosity, greed, and other dysfunctional behaviours;

> ➢ To develop the following business leadership attributes: social intelligence, emotional intelligence, cultural intelligence, ecological intelligence, geography intelligence, and religious intelligence;
> ➢ To restore societal trust in business leaders. For this, new relationships that are dear to society need to be developed as a whole to deliver positive intergenerational results, that is, to deliver robust sustainability as an organ of society by applying the Social Contract with Business.

What kind of business for such a society?

> ➢ To cultivate a business culture that understands that a stable societal environment is a prerequisite for sustained profitability, that is, that the firm is not the whole, but a part of the whole;
> ➢ To cultivate a business culture of winning through the creative application of multidisciplinary knowledge, global learning, and learning from history, that is, to seek competitive advantage outside the narrow confines of the firm's niche;
> ➢ To develop a corporate decision-making process that considers the holistic context of issues, and to assess it from different perspectives and from different modes of thought before coming to any conclusion, that is, to use both linear and holistic thinking;
> ➢ To develop an enterprise-wide dual capability to manage in both a local and a global environment, in both a high and a low technology environment, in both a first and a developing world environment, and at both the top and bottom ends of the human pyramid;

> ➤ To develop enterprise-wide entrepreneurial services capabilities in order to deliver on the key drivers of sustained business success, namely, entrepreneurial versatility, trust-building ingenuity, entrepreneurial ambition, entrepreneurial judgement, entrepreneurial innovation, entrepreneurial implementation, intrapreneurial operations, and entrepreneurial stewardship.

What kind of leader for such a business?

> ➤ To cultivate a global mindset, oriented towards a WOIG future;
> ➤ To develop the ability to make holistic decisions that advances the cause of a WOIG;
> ➤ To cultivate a personal ethic of responsibility towards a WOIG future; and
> ➤ To develop an educational paradigm that is aimed at educating a specific kind of leader for a specific kind of future, that is, a WOIG leader for a WOIG future.

You may be tempted to consider the above as a list of individual tasks. You may even be tempted to condense it to a simplistic 3-step approach to deliver a WOIG. Please do not revert back to magical mantras or slogans to solve complex global issues—this is the domain of management witchdoctors!

The above list of *kairos* events constitutes a new whole. All the parts of the whole are individually and collectively either contributing to, or undermining the successful turnaround to a WOIG. The WOIG business leadership's challenge is to set this whole in motion, and then to keep it sustained in ever increased waves of effectiveness and expanded areas of influence—whether you are a global institute such as the World Economic Forum, a government, a MNC, a local enterprise, or an individual.

To restate the above in practical strategy implementation terms: *mastery of this whole, structures your turnaround strategy to a WOIG for success, or the individual parts of this whole are the pre-control measures to ensure sustained success.*

Personal empowerment:

- ✓ Key learnings: . . .
- ✓ Action plan: . . .

Language

In order to understand, think, and act in the new WOIG, a new vocabulary is needed that is in contrast with today's language of the WODG. This new vocabulary is analogous to the awesome discovery of the microchip that drives our modern way of life. Alternatively said, modern life is not driven by the steam engine (i.e. yesterday's language!).

Likewise, the awesome power of wisdom, love, and courage as words directs WOIG business leadership. This powerful new vocabulary drives historic acts of business leadership, as was illustrated with twelve examples from around the world in Chapter 6. This new vocabulary will also empower you to apply small acts of leadership when confronted by someone who:

> does not hear the voices calling for change from around the world (Chapter 1);
> does not understand why change is necessary (Chapter 2);
> does not wish to seek the wisdom from today's leaders and thinkers (Chapter 3);
> finds the Socratic dialogue boring (Chapter 4);
> resists change, despite evidence to the contrary (Chapter 5);
> laughs at the new language for a new world (Chapter 6);
> misses the power of the Social Contract with Business (Chapter 7);
> misses the change of mindset happening in the case studies (Chapter 8); and
> does not understand why leadership blind spots are a problem (Chapter 9).

Personal empowerment:

✓ Key learnings: . . .
✓ Action plan: . . .

The Social Contract with Business

The Social Contract with Business was introduced as a business case that delivers humanity's global sustainability mandate. The business case consists of business' responsibility directed . . . towards itself is to be an organ of society; towards its direct stakeholders is to be sustainable; towards the earth is its alignment with the earth's finite nature; towards the global commons is to be a co-custodian thereof; towards society is to be a co-architect of a healthy society; towards democracy is to protect its own operating space; towards government is its alignment with government priorities; and towards transnational crime is to eliminate its role and influence.

Personal empowerment:

- ✓ Key learnings: . . .
- ✓ Action plan: . . .

Entrepreneurial services

During the Socratic dialogue, the Global Icons have unknowingly reconfirmed and re-contextualised Edith Penrose's 'Theory of the Growth of the Firm'. The original four drivers of the sustainability of the firm have been expanded to eight termed entrepreneurial services:

Entrepreneurial versatility: Moving beyond management and technical competence to build a WOIG enterprise as an organ of a WOIG society;

Trust-building ingenuity: Convincing a sceptical audience about the merits of the enterprise's intent to turn around to a WOIG, and then to invest in it;

Entrepreneurial ambition: Moving away from the comfort zone of destructive globalisation towards building a new WOIG-kind future;

Entrepreneurial judgement: Having the ability to make holistic decisions through analysis and wisdom to advance the cause of good for all stakeholders;

Entrepreneurial innovation: Having the ability to innovate in technologies, education, mindsets, and value-propositions necessary for a turn-around to a WOIG;

Entrepreneurial implementation: Having the ability to master the art, science, and craft of implementation without compromising on quality, time, budget, and integrity;

Intrapreneurial operations: Having the ability to exploit technologies and opportunities to optimise the firm's assets towards delivering sustained prosperity to a WOIG society; and

Entrepreneurial stewardship: Having the wisdom, love, and courage to exert path-breaking leadership to apply the Social Contract with Business as an intergenerational business case.

These eight long-term success drivers of the WOIG business need to be mastered on an individual and enterprise-wide basis.

Personal empowerment:

   ✓ Key learnings: . . .
   ✓ Action plan: . . .

Kairos (καιρός) capabilities

The premise is that a global mindset and an ability to make holistic decisions are *the* pre-requisites to lead to a WOIG—the educational *kairos* events. After mastering these two competences, you will have broken the glass ceiling towards higher modes of thinking and doing. The specific subjects to be mastered for each competence are given in Chapter 12.

Let's now discuss each competence in more detail:

A global mindset is defined[1] as 'a highly complex cognitive structure characterised by an openness to and articulation of multiple cultural and strategic realities on both global and local levels, and the cognitive ability to mediate and integrate across this multiplicity. It has three complementary traits: (a) an openness to and an awareness of multiple spheres of meaning and action; (b) complex representation and articulation of cultural and strategic dynamics; and (c) mediation and integration of ideals and actions both globally and locally.'

For a global mindset, the specific outcome should be a mindset oriented towards the values of, and the turn-around to, a WOIG. The evolutionary growth from a local mindset to a global mindset is depicted in Figure 10.1. You will go through four distinct phases of personal growth over a three to five year period, namely, **A:** Being a 'defender' of your local turf and narrow mindset—all external influences are considered either inferior or hostile to your own world; **B:** Being a 'controller'—cautiously observing the world, but rationalise why your world is the best; **C:** Being an 'explorer'—discovering the wealth of the world's wisdoms and practices, and even start experimenting with it in your world; **D:** Being an 'integrator'—applying the local and the global to gain new value, while remaining authentic and true to yourself.

Figure 10.1 The evolution of a global mindset

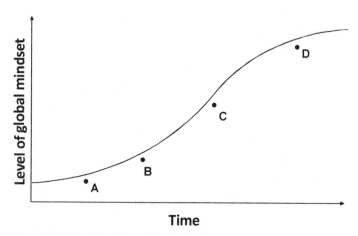

Source: Kedia and Mukherji[2], adjusted by the author.

For holistic decision-making, the specific outcome should be an ability to exercise entrepreneurial judgement to advance the ideals of a WOIG. This ability calls for intellectual flexibility and to work on all four levels of decision-making as outlined in Figure 10.2. For increased holistic decision-making prowess, you need to break three glass ceilings to gain access to the highest mode of thought; you need to be able to work across the full spectrum of modes of thought; you need wisdom to understand the value and limitations of each mode of thought; you need wisdom to incorporate inputs from all modes of thought into a decision; and lastly, you need to control your ego should you need to change an earlier decision in the face of new evidence or insight.

Figure 10.2 Breaking three glass ceilings

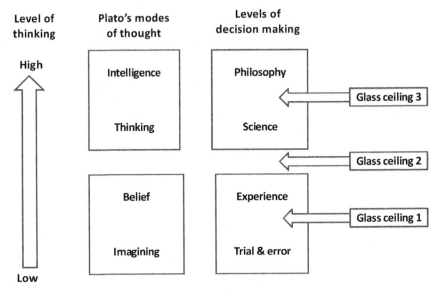

Holistic decision making covers all modes of thought

Source: Stumpf and Abel[3], adjusted by the author.

Personal empowerment:

- ✓ Key learnings: . . .
- ✓ Action plan: . . .

Doing capabilities

The premise is that hard skills are essential to design, build, and sustain the WOIG enterprise—it's only a jelly fish that has soft tissue! The specific subjects to be mastered as leader-in-practice competences are given in Chapter 12.

In addition to mastering the above leadership-in-practice competences, the WOIG leader needs to develop a sixth sense to learn from the global experiences from his or her own, and other firms. Business science has the world as its laboratory of examples of excellence and of disasters—why reinvent the wheel if you can learn from others? These learnings can be replicated directly or in a manner that suits the firm (unless, of course, if protected by intellectual property laws). Table 10.2 provides an example of how such global learnings can be structured into a powerful and unique core competence for the firm.

Table 10.2 Global learning matrix

Leadership responsibility domain		Leadership area of competence	
Social Contract with Business	Example	**Entrepreneurial services**	Example
Towards business itself	1	Entrepreneurial versatility	9
Towards direct stakeholders	2	Trust-building ingenuity	10
Towards the earth	3	Entrepreneurial ambition	11
Towards the global commons	4	Entrepreneurial judgement	12
Towards society	5	Entrepreneurial innovation	13
Towards democracy	6	Entrepreneurial implementation	14
Towards politics	7	Intrapreneurial operations	15
Towards transnational crime	8	Entrepreneurial stewardship	16

Source: Author.

The examples below are not intended to be a definitive set of global best practice, but an indication of the richness of global learning:

Global learning 1: From ExxonMobil—the pursuit of *integrated* solutions to build wealth in an environmentally responsible manner.

Global learning 2: From Anglo American plc—their annual US$10 billion procurement budget to further *develop* local communities' ability to produce quality goods and services.

Global learning 3: From the carbon-credit market—financial *incentives* to reduce pollution.

Global learning 4: From Google and Wikipedia—to make knowledge *available* to humanity at low cost on open source platforms.

Global learning 5: From the SSI Engineering Company in South Africa—their engineers empower *local* school children with their Saturday Schools in mathematics and science.

Global learning 6: The many business leaders who *support* AVAAZ, the global social-media watchdog over democracy and responsible business practice.

Global learning 7: From the Industrial and Commercial Bank of China—the *alignment* of business objectives with government's priorities.

Global learning 8: From Business against Crime, South Africa—an example of how the formal business community *joins* the state to combat local and transnational crime.

Global learning 9: The *amazing* story of Nokia's conversion from a local timber company in Sweden to a mammoth cellular phone MNC.

Global learning 10: From the UN's new US$300 billion Green Fund—watch this initiative to see how they *secure* funding for new green projects.

Global learning 11: From the Polyus Gold Company—the *first* mining company to introduce a formal and transparent corporate governance policy in Russia.

Global learning 12: From the Grameen Bank in Bangladesh—their *judgment* to grant loans to micro-entrepreneurs who have no security to offer as collateral.

Global learning 13: From all energy companies—their ability to *innovate* energy saving technologies as well as the pursuit of green energy technologies.

Global learning 14: From Fluor Daniel—their ability to *implement* cross-border projects.

Global learning 15: From General Electric's 'ecomagination' corporate *culture*—their ability to use their employees' creativity to invent new green practices and products.

Global learning 16: From all the firms mentioned above—all working towards stewardship as a business case, that is a *delightful* work-in-progress.

Personal empowerment:

✓ Key learnings: . . .
✓ Action plan: . . .

In conclusion, you have been given a comprehensive and step-by-step application guide to sharpen your competences to become a WOIG business leader, and once you feel that you have sufficiently mastered all the building blocks, then to make yourself available to mentor a colleague(s) or a young business leader(s) in order to set your own virtuous cycle in motion.

In the next chapter, I will leverage on your new competences to apply the Social Contract with Business in SmartCo, a company still stuck in the WODG.

---

[1]   Levy, O., Beechler, S., Taylor, S. and Boyaciller, N. A. 2007. 'What we talk about when we talk about 'global mindset': Managerial cognition in multinational corporations', *Journal of International Business Studies*, 38: 231-258.

[2]   Kedia, B. L. and Mukherji, A., 1999. 'Global managers: Developing a mindset for global competitiveness', *Journal of World Business*, 34(3): 230-251. Adjusted by the author.

[3]   Stumpf, E. S. and Abel, D. C. 2002. *Elements of Philosophy: An Introduction*, 4th ed. New York: McGraw Hill.

CHAPTER 11

APPLICATION GUIDELINES FOR BUSINESS ENTERPRISES

The objective of this chapter is to guide business leaders towards applying the Social Contract with Business within their own enterprises.

This will be done in a typical strategy workshop format. In a step-by-step manner the rationale and methodology of each application guideline will be introduced. Generic strategic planning templates will be used, which you can of course adjust to suit your own situation.

The setting for the strategy workshop is as follows:

SmartCo, a fictitious Australian-based MNC, has been introduced in the case studies of Chapter 8. In this chapter, the case study continues . . .

SmartCo's Chairman, CEO, and three global business managers (John, Rajeshwari, and Karlheinz) have just finished a provisional assessment of SmartCo relative to the Social Contract with Business' success criteria, and all are in a state of shock as they looked at the irrefutable bad news as depicted in Figure 11.1. The firm's sustainability is at extreme risk because 50 per cent of the success criteria are in need of strategic intervention, and the firm makes absolutely no contribution to deliver humanity's global sustainability mandate—in fact, SmartCo is typical of a firm doing business in a WODG.

The situation now is that the executive team has decided to set a strategic process in motion to turn around to a WOIG by applying the Social Contract with Business at SmartCo. The strategy workshop commences with a formal letter of invitation . . .

Figure 11.1 Profile of SmartCo's current Social Contract with Business

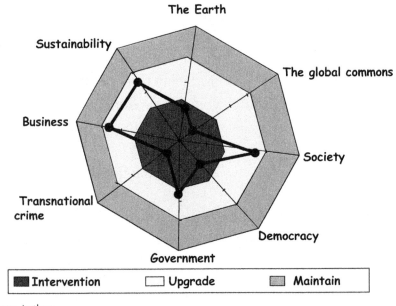

Source: Author.

An Invitation to Attend a Strategy Workshop

To: SmartCo's strategic shareholders, executive directors, and senior management.

Rationale: *A corporate turn-around to a WOIG needs the individual and collective commitment from all key decision-makers. In this way, buy-in is assured from the beginning of the turn-around process.*

Objective: To apply the Social Contract with Business at SmartCo.

Rationale: *SmartCo's reputation of its destructive business models and practices are increasingly unacceptable to its stakeholders. Consequently, the corporate mood is increasingly that delivering on humanity's global sustainability mandate is the new reality.*

Type of strategy workshop: Strategic decision-making

Rationale: *Prior to this workshop there would have been many informal conversations and lobbying that SmartCo needs to reposition itself within a WOIG. This workshop is now to formalise the new corporate mood, and to take strategic decisions that will reposition SmartCo as a WOIG firm.*

Date and venue: Five days at Tranquil Place

Rationale: *Optimal time is required at a venue conducive to a meeting of minds and hearts. Sufficient time is required for debate, buy-in, reflection, decision-making, reality-checking, and tactical implementation planning.*

External invitees: Eminent Persons A and B

Rationale: *To stimulate creative thinking, to provide an external view, to provide a hedge against group think, to challenge assumptions and decisions, and to move the conversation forward in a balanced, positive, and realistic manner.*

Pre-reading:

Jopie Coetzee, 2012. *The Social Contract with Business: beyond the quest for global sustainability.* London: Xlibris Publishers.

Rationale: *The invitees should all have been exposed to the same background reading in order to create a common platform from where to launch the strategic conversation.*

Agenda:

1. Reflection.
2. Commitment.
3. Scenario planning.
4. Gap analysis.
5. Reflection.
6. Strategic questions.
7. Global learnings.
8. Strategic implementation planning.
9. Reflection.
10. Communication to stakeholders.

Rationale: *The agenda needs to be covered in the style of a strategic conversation using the consensus-seeking nominal group technique where the invitees debate issues openly and robustly during a facilitated process before decisions are taken.*

Signed	*Signed*	*Signed*
Controlling Shareholder	**Chairperson**	**Chief Executive Officer**

The Strategy Workshop

Agenda Point 1: Reflection

An optimal beginning would be a moment of silent meditation in order to connect with one's inner voice and higher faculties of thinking. Thereafter, each invitee reflects on his or her thoughts about the objective of the strategic conversation in an open forum through a facilitated process.

The key outcome of this agenda point is to get a whole-brain (balanced) understanding of the issues at stake, that is, the visionary issues (top right brain), the analytic issues (top left brain), the implementation issues (bottom left brain), and lastly the relationship issues (bottom right brain).

Agenda Point 2: Commitment

In a facilitated process, each invitee signs-off on the understanding of and a personal commitment to the definition of the Social Contract with Business.

In the next facilitated session, the consequent key risks and opportunities for SmartCo are identified and ranked, using a simple layout as per Table 11.1.

Table 11.1 SmartCo's strategic risks and opportunities

Implications for SmartCo by taking up the Social Contract with Business	Risks	Opportunities
Internal environment		
Market environment		
Macro environment		
Business development		
External stakeholders		

Source: Author.

The key outcome of this agenda point is a personal and a shared commitment to the Social Contract with Business, and the acceptance of the consequent key risks and opportunities.

Agenda Point 3: Scenario planning

The first step is to determine SmartCo's relative position between a WODG and a WOIG. Doing this requires agreement on: a) the distribution of SmartCo's business model between a WODG and a WOIG; and b) the dominant moral fibre of SmartCo. To guide this trade-off discussion four probable global scenario game boards are given in Figure 11.2

For the purpose of this step, the following assumptions are made: SmartCo's business model is assumed to be 80 per cent in a WODG and 20 per cent in a WOIG, and consequently that SmartCo's moral fibre is that of an amoral firm.

The challenge therefore is to set strategic actions in motion so that its business model is one hundred per cent positioned in a WOIG and that its dominant moral fibre is that of a moral firm.

Figure 11.2 SmartCo's relative position in its evolution to a WOIG

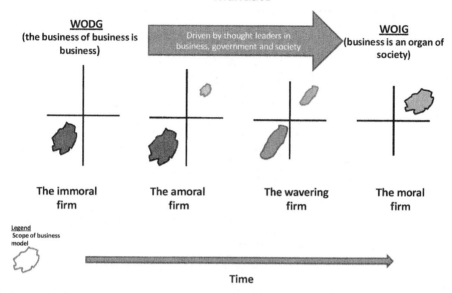

The evolutionary road to deliver humanity's global sustainability mandate

WODG
(the business of business is business)

Driven by thought leaders in business, government and society

WOIG
(business is an organ of society)

The immoral firm   The amoral firm   The wavering firm   The moral firm

Legend
Scope of business model

Time

Source: Author.

Secondly, SmartCo's firm-specific scenario game board with the two key variables that will shape its future, namely, the X-axis as its competitiveness in a WOIG market and the Y-axis as its quality of contribution to humanity's global sustainability mandate (See Figure 11.3).

For the purpose of this agenda point, it is assumed that SmartCo is in the 'loser's circle' quadrant of the firm-specific scenario game board. In scenario planning terms this implies that SmartCo's current status is as follows:

> ➢ along the X-axis: Low competitiveness in a WOIG market (whilst probably being highly competitive in a WODG market):

> ➤ along the Y-axis: A low level of contribution to humanity's global sustainability mandate.

Figure 11.3 SmartCo's scenario game board

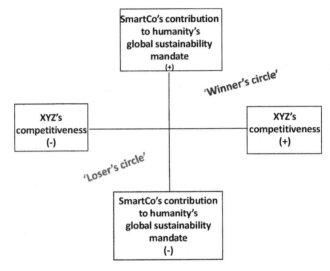

Source: Author.

The key outcome of this agenda point is a shared understanding of where SmartCo is currently positioned, and what its end-status should be. This sets the scene for the next agenda point, namely the gap analysis and strategic actions to be taken to close the gap.

Agenda Point 4: Gap analysis

This agenda point calls for five facilitated sessions, namely to assess:

> ➤ to what extent SmartCo contributes to humanity's global sustainability mandate (Table 11.3);
> ➤ the quality of SmartCo's leadership responsibility as required by the Social Contract with Business (Table 11.4);

> ➤ the quality of SmartCo's entrepreneurial services as drivers of a WOIG firm (Table 11.5);
> ➤ the quality of SmartCo's executives competences (Table 11.6); and lastly
> ➤ The extent to which blind spots have been eliminated by SmartCo's executives (Table 11.7).

The scoring rules that apply for the gap analysis for the above five facilitated sessions are given in Table 11.2:

Table 11.2 Scoring rules and types of intervention plans

Score	Description of contribution or quality	Level of intervention plans
10	Strongly positive	Ongoing monitoring
5	Good	Management intervention
0	Neutral	CEO intervention
−5	Pathetic	Board intervention
−10	Strongly negative	Shareholder intervention

Source: Author.

Table 11.3 SmartCo's current contribution to humanity's global sustainability mandate

SmartCo	The various elements of humanity's global sustainability mandate (note the duality within each element)	Score	Action plan
Vision and Mission Statement and/or Chairman's and CEO's letters in the latest Annual Report	**What kind of world?** A WOIG where systemic poverty has been permanently removed and . . . where humanity's broad security is assured.		
	What kind of society? A society that finds its greatness in protecting both its humanity and . . . its economy as a whole.		
	What kind of business? World-class enterprises—financially robust across economic cycles, and with . . . global stewardship as the dominant business logic		
	What kind of business leader? Global leaders with an ability to envision the WOIG, and . . . then to lead thereto in an entrepreneurial and path-breaking manner exerting . . . leadership qualities associated with the Golden Rule of Humanity.		

Note: As scoring criteria, ask yourself to what extent SmartCo contributes to each of the respective 18 *kairos* events.

Source: Author.

Table 11.4 SmartCo's current quality of leadership as per the Social Contract with Business

Quality of leadership directed . . .	Score	Action plan
towards itself is to be an organ of society;		
towards its direct stakeholders is to be sustainable;		
towards the Earth is its alignment with the Earth's finite nature;		
towards the global commons is to be a co-custodian thereof;		
towards society is to be a co-architect of a healthy society;		
towards democracy is to protect its own operating space;		
towards government is its alignment with government priorities; and		
towards transnational crime is to eliminate its role and influence.		

Source: Author.

Table 11.5 SmartCo's current quality of entrepreneurial services as drivers of a WOIG firm

Entrepreneurial services requirement	Score	Action plan
Entrepreneurial versatility: moving beyond management and technical competence to build a WOIG enterprise as an organ of a WOIG society.		
Trust-building ingenuity: convincing a sceptical audience about the merits of the enterprise's intent to turn-around to a WOIG, and to invest in it.		
Entrepreneurial ambition: moving away from the comfort zone of destructive globalisation towards building a new WOIG-kind future.		
Entrepreneurial judgement: having the ability to make holistic decisions through analysis and wisdom to advance the cause of good for all stakeholders.		
Entrepreneurial innovation: having the ability to innovate in technologies, education, mindsets, and value-propositions necessary for a turn-around to a WOIG.		

Entrepreneurial implementation: having the ability to master the art, science, and craft of implementation without compromising on quality, time, budget and integrity.		
Intrapreneurial operations: having the ability to exploit technologies and opportunities to optimise the firm's assets towards delivering sustained prosperity to a WOIG society.		
Entrepreneurial stewardship: having the wisdom, love, and courage to exert path-breaking leadership to apply the Social Contract with Business as an intergenerational business case.		

Source: Author.

Figure 11.6 Current competencies of SmartCo's key decision-makers

Leadership competence domains	Score	Action plan
Global mindset		
Holistic decision-making		
Craft wealth		
Build wealth		
Manage wealth		

Source: Author.

Figure 11.7 The extent to which SmartCo's executives eliminated each blind spot

Blind spots prohibiting application	Score	Action plan
Ignoring minor voices at your own peril		
The cowardly silencing of the inner voice		
The madness of aspiring downwards		
The daftness of negative belief perseverance		
The tragedy of reality confusion		
Wisdom is for philosophers only		
Love is for lovers only		
Courage is for dead heroes only		
The sadness of linear thinking in a holistic world		
The foolishness of entrenched fallacies		
The regret of missed small opportunities		

Source: Author.

The key outcome of this agenda point is a shared understanding of size and nature of the gaps between the current reality and the end-state, and also what strategic actions are required to fill the gap.

Agenda Point 5: Reflecting

At this stage of the strategic conversation, SmartCo is now poised to make strategic choices on how to close the strategic gap and how to manage the consequent risks and opportunities. Therefore, it would be prudent to pause here, and to reflect on the enormity of what has happened so far. Can SmartCo's Social Contract with Business' profile really be turned around from the profile's negative shape as in Figure 11.1 to the profile's ideal shape as depicted in Figure 7.3?

In addition to an internal reflection by the invitees, it will be prudent at this stage to invite a few respected stakeholders to comment on the strategic conversation thus far. Such stakeholders may be strategic investors, strategic customers, strategic service providers and strategic personnel from SmartCo.

The key outcomes of this agenda point are a reality check and to get reconfirmation of the invitees' commitment to align SmartCo with the Social Contract with Business.

Agenda Point 6: Strategic questions

SmartCo's strategic objective is crystal clear—it needs to become an ethical firm in a WOIG on the global scenario game board (Figure

11.2), and it needs to enter the 'winner's circle' on the firm-specific scenario game board (Figure 11.3). For this, SmartCo needs to consider both its entry strategy into a WOIG and its divestment strategy from a WODG. Therefore, SmartCo needs to consider at least the following strategic questions:

> Business development—into a WOIG, and out of a WODG?
> Which growth pathway—a quantum leap or incremental steps?
> What scale—the entire SmartCo or one division at a time?
> What tempo—fast (1-3 years) or slow (7-10 years)?
> Key resources required for implementation?
> Acquire new competitive advantages?
> Management re-education?
> Innovation priorities?

The key outcome of this agenda point is the design criteria for implementation planning.

Agenda Point 7: Global learnings

Before implementation planning commences, it would be prudent to scan the external business environment to identify examples of excellence and pitfalls from competitors and related industries. Table 11.8 gives an example of a structured approach for global learning.

Table 11.8 Global learning matrix for SmartCo

Leadership responsibility		Leadership competency	
Social Contract with Business	Example	**Entrepreneurial services**	Example
Towards business itself		Entrepreneurial versatility	
Towards direct stakeholders		Trust-building ingenuity	
Towards the earth		Entrepreneurial ambition	
Towards the global commons		Entrepreneurial judgement	
Towards society		Entrepreneurial innovation	
Towards democracy		Entrepreneurial implementation	
Towards politics		Intrapreneurial operations	
Towards global crime		Entrepreneurial stewardship	

Source: Author.

The key outcome is to learn from the positive and negative experiences as well as the wisdom of enterprises which have already embarked on the journey to a WOIG. The scene has now been set for implementation planning

---

Agenda Point 8: Implementation planning

For the purpose of this discussion, the following implementation timetable for the Social Contract with Business to be fully operational is assumed to be as per Table 11.9.

The reason for such a phased and decentralised (cascaded) approach is to secure buy-in across the organisation, and to spread the learning curve and risks over a reasonable time.

Figure 11.9 Implementation scheduling of the Social Contract with Business at SmartCo

SmartCo corporate entity	Years (to become fully operational #1)	Champion
Board	2	Chairman
Overall turnaround strategy	10	CEO
Functional departments	3	Heads of Departments
Operations:		
Business Unit 1	3	General Manager
Business Units 2-5	5	General Managers
Business Units 6-10	10	General Managers
Project development:		
New projects (Capex < US$10 million)	3	Project Managers
New projects (Capex < US$100 million)	5	Project Managers
New projects (Capex < US$1000 million)	10	Project Managers
Special projects:		
Upscale SmartCo's ability to innovate #2	1	CEO
New project pipeline in 'winner's circle'	5	Business Development Manager
Secure finance for SmartCo's new ventures	2	Finance Manager
Re-education of management team	2	Personnel Manager
Re-education of customers	2	Marketing manager

Note:

#1: Fully operational implies closing the strategic gaps as identified in Agenda Point 4.

#2: Upscale SmartCo's ability to innovate implies technological as well as cultural and mindset innovations.

Source: Author.

The outcome of this agenda point is that each champion needs to know what is to be done in order to draft his or her own detailed turnaround plan.

Agenda Point 9: Reflection

This is the final pause to reflect and to reconfirm shared commitment, and to fine-tune the strategic tactics of an integrated turnaround plan to align SmartCo with the Social Contract with Business.

Agenda Point 10: Communication to stakeholders

For SmartCo, a MNC working in sixty countries, such a communiqué will be a trade-off between the risks and opportunities identified in Table 11.1. Such a public announcement will set-off immense entrepreneurial forces working either for or against SmartCo. This will be a time of great WOIG business leadership.

The outcome of this agenda point is a public commitment that SmartCo has signed the Social Contract with Business . . . and, that it intends to deliver on humanity's global sustainability mandate.

No doubt, the market and society will hold SmartCo accountable.

Let's just remember that the application of the Social Contract with Business in your enterprise is not done in isolation from other in-house best-practices, competitive advantages, and core competences.

CHAPTER 12

APPLICATION GUIDELINES FOR
BUSINESS LEADERSHIP EDUCATION

The objective of this chapter is to provide business leaders, business school deans, and academics with research-based[1] application guidelines for total business school transformation in order to develop a WOIG business leader.

I will focus on the general MBA qualification, because it is the world's premier post graduate management qualification. This qualification sets the educational standard and quality benchmarks for management and business education. In particular this standard is set by those graduate business schools that are globally accredited by the EFMD (European Foundation for Management Development). Local accreditation organisations also contribute to such quality assurance (e.g., in the USA it's the AACSB—The Association to Advance Collegiate Schools of Business).

All, or part, of the MBA is also offered around the world by a myriad of corporate universities, management faculties, training institutes, and executive development programmes. Therefore, all institutions involved in the development of business leaders may benefit from this chapter in one way or the other.

The chapter is structured around the following themes:

1. Why today's MBA educational paradigm is not fit for purpose anymore;
2. The postmodern MBA's educational paradigm, *conscientisation* ('postmodern' simply means 'beyond' what is today considered as 'modern');
3. A blueprint for a business school offering the postmodern MBA qualification; and
4. Implementation considerations.

Regarding why today's MBA educational paradigm is not fit for purpose anymore:

Today's MBA applies one of the following educational paradigms[2]:

'Functions of business': where the MBA curriculum mimics the various functions of business, such as operations management, personnel management, financial management, and marketing management;

'Input-output': where the MBA curriculum is populated by many ad-hoc and unrelated subjects as requested by many different industries; or

'Character development': where the MBA focuses mainly on leadership and charisma competences.

These educational paradigms became the holy grail of management education since the 1950s and are based upon amoral business ethics, capitalism, linear (silo, scientific) thinking, and a Western canon of knowledge. Organic changes over time did occur, but only as a belated result of external events, such as: (a) The Porter and McKibben Report[3] in 1988, which recommended that MBA curriculum content should be more integrated and inclusive of doing global business; (b) the fall of the Berlin Wall in 1989 introduced an awareness of other canons of knowledge than Western; (c) the corporate scandals of the 1990s, such as Enron, introduced ethics and corporate governance subjects into the MBA curriculum; (d) the global warming discourse introduced sustainability and green subjects; (e) the food and economic crises in the 2000s caused a rethink of economic delivery modes and the role of business in society.

Sadly, the world's premier management qualification, the MBA, has become a victim of its own success, stuck below a glass ceiling.

Why, when the MBA has had such phenomenal success following its transition from a pre-modern to a modern qualification in the 1950s, is it in this predicament? Simple. The pace of change in the global business environment has outpaced changes to the MBA.

The *Economist*[4] compares today's geopolitical and socio-economic forces with the Industrial Revolution of 200 years ago in the way they are shaping a new world. Except that two centuries ago only a third of the global population was affected; today, nearly the entire population of the world will be.

Business schools initially responded to this tsunami of global change with incremental adjustments to the MBA curriculum as given above and depicted in Figure 12.1. Such a strategic approach is typical of an industry follower, which is not acceptable for an academic institute that is supposed to provide intellectual leadership to the business community.

The economic crisis of 2008 (that's still ongoing in 2012) is a stark reminder that the point of diminishing returns has been reached in attempting to make an outdated educational paradigm fit-for-purpose through small curriculum changes or novel pedagogical techniques. But business schools continue to deliver this re-jigged MBA successfully—paradoxically, a case of implementing the wrong strategy very effectively.

See Figures A1 and A2 for a graphical depiction of the academic discourse on the future of the MBA and a new agenda for the discourse on the future of the MBA respectively, which are fully described in Appendix A.

If the MBA is to reposition itself as the leading management qualification in a new world order, the glass ceiling needs to be broken to let in higher modes of thought—the domain of the postmodern MBA.

The glass ceiling is MBA curriculum designers' inability to answer (or fear of answering) the calls for change made by eminent scholars over the past twenty-five years, asking questions such as 'What is the role of management and business in society?', 'What is a business for?', 'What is the end-purpose of a firm's vision?', 'What global scenario contextualises the firm's vision?', 'What dominant logic is required to eradicate poverty at the bottom of the human pyramid?', 'Why have business schools failed themselves and society?'

Regarding the postmodern MBA's educational paradigm:

Beyond the glass ceiling, the world of *conscientisation* awaits business educators to arrive[5].

Conscientisation is the educational paradigm that aims to develop business leaders, capable of applying the Social Contract with Business as a means to deliver a specific WOIG kind of future. This educational challenge is to develop a practical conscience-based critical awareness of the values and ideals of a WOIG. The postmodern MBA's educational paradigm stands in stark contrast to today's modern MBA as depicted in Figure 12.1.

Figure 12.1 The contrast between a modern and a postmodern MBA

Modern MBA				Postmodern MBA
Old world	**Transition**	**Glass ceiling**		**WOIG**
Western canon Capitalism 'Business is the whole'				West, East & South canon Eco-economic conservationism 'Business is an organ of society'
Amoral ←	**Schools of management educational paradigms**			**→ Moral**
Functions of business Input – output Character building	Green			*Conscientização*
External drivers of change Ford: Foundation Reports – 1950's Porter & McKibben report – 1988 Enron Berlin Wall Global warming & ecological degradation Food & Economic crises of 2008-09 Increased social activism – 'no Planet B to go to'- 2010 Political economic crisis: Jasmine revolut on - 2011				Internal driver of change A practical conscience-based critical awareness towards delivering a specific kind of future, namely: *humanity's global sustainability mandate to its business leaders*

Source: Author.

The other unique distinguishing features of the postmodern MBA are that:

> ➢ it is based on an original and research-based revision of the MBA, which yields a new educational context, a new vocabulary as well as guidelines for a new canon of knowledge for business education;
> ➢ it anticipates the next fundamental deflection in the evolution of the MBA, namely a new world order reflecting the rebalancing of global economic and political power as well as the emergence of a holistic society;
> ➢ it is aligned with the aspirations of humanity, embracing Western, Eastern, and Southern wisdom, values, and knowledge;
> ➢ it is driven by an internal conscience-based ethic of responsibility to a WOIG future;
> ➢ it aims to provide intellectual leadership to responsible business; and
> ➢ it is aligned with the educational building blocks as per Table 10.1, each of which is another distinguishing feature (i.e., fundamental values, *Kosoryoku*; turnaround strategy to a WOIG, new language, Social Contract with Business, entrepreneurial services, *Kairos* capabilities, and doing capabilities).

Regarding the canon on knowledge for the postmodern MBA, readers need to note the following good news: (a) no matter how modern the MBA becomes, the basic principles of management remains a constant factor namely, planning, organising, leading, and control of business functions—just like anatomy, which remains a constant factor, no matter how specialised a medical doctor becomes; and, (b) the new competences required for the postmodern MBA are already available in the broad scope of management science, but unfortunately not yet recognised (or being oblivious of, or not being tolerated) by mainline academia and, consequently not yet documented in lecturing material—this is another symptom of being stuck below the glass ceiling.

In order to conclude the perspective of the conscientisation educational paradigm, I want to give you a longitudinal perspective as depicted in Figure 12.2. Do you remember that it was Gary Hamel who said that today we can imagine what we want and then plan backward from there towards what we should be doing today, rather than simply to plan forward from our history?

Likewise, the conscientisation educational paradigm aims to develop business leaders who can deliver a WOIG future—not as a function of imagination, but as a function of a well researched end-result of humanity's global sustainability mandate.

Doing just this is the new reality for responsible business schools!

Figure 12.2 The educational journey of a postmodern MBA student

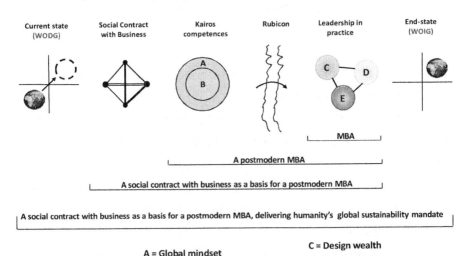

A = Global mindset
B = Holistic decision making

C = Design wealth
D = Build wealth
E = Manage wealth

Source: Author.

Regarding a blueprint for a business school offering the postmodern MBA qualification:

VISION: (what kind of MBA graduates do we wish to produce?)

Business leaders who can apply the Social Contract with Business.

Rationale: *To sculpt leaders who can lead the turnaround from a world of destructive globalisation to a world of inclusive globalisation—on the global stage, and in any country and in any sector of human endeavour.*

END-Purpose: (so what if the vision is achieved?)

To heed humanity's global sustainability mandate to its leaders, namely to deliver:

— *a WOIG, where systemic poverty has been permanently removed and where humanity's broad security is assured* (**i.e., a dual end-purpose of the firm's vision**); *requiring . . .*
— *a society that finds its greatness in the courage of protecting both its humanity and its economy as a whole* (**i.e., a dual end-purpose for responsible business leadership**); *requiring . . .*
— *a world-class business—financially robust across economic cycles, with global stewardship as the dominant business logic* (**i.e., dual success criteria for the firm's business model**); *requiring . . .*
— *a business leader with the ability to envision the WOIG, and then to lead thereto in an entrepreneurial and path-breaking*

manner exerting leadership qualities associated with the Golden Rule of Humanity (**i.e., business leadership anchored in wisdom, love, and courage**).

Rationale: *Sustained sustainability for the firm can only be attained by delivering on the above mandate—this is the raison d'être of business as an organ of society. This also provides for a meaningful purpose for business leadership as a profession.*

MISSION: (so how do you intend to deliver on your vision?)

Educational paradigm: *conscientisation*

Rationale: *This educational paradigm aims at sculpting MBA graduates to deliver a specific kind of future, that is, a WOIG future. The educational challenge is to develop a practical conscience-based critical awareness of the values and ideals of a WOIG.*

Entry requirements

Any bachelor's degree; and

Prior learning of at least a first year university qualification in:

- ○ Economics; and
- ○ Reasoning through words, such as philosophy or literature; and
- ○ Reasoning through numbers, such as mathematics or accounting.
- ○ The student should already be a full-time employee or entrepreneur.

Rationale: *(a) to attract gifted men and women to lead the top echelons of any business, societal, or government enterprise; (b) this kind of prior learning prepares the mind for broad-based intellectual agility and higher cognitive abilities; and (c) the MBA student must already be a working adult in order to understand the theoretical grounding of business science.*

Curriculum design principles

Overall structure

For the sake of completeness, the growth path of a WOIG leader given in Chapter 10 is repeated here as a guide to structure the curriculum, either as:

- an educational event over a specific period (e.g., two years), or
- as an educational process over a leadership development timeline, of, for example, five years. In this case, formal education is provided for three months per year, with mentored on-the-job training for nine months per year. Such a leadership development pipeline[6] may provide for the following distinct phases of maturity: managing self, managing people, managing managers, managing a company, and managing companies.

Table 12.1 The overall curriculum structure of the postmodern MBA

BUILDING BLOCKS	OUTCOMES
Doing capabilities	Design, build and maintain prosperity
(leadership-in-practice capabilities)	Global learning
Kairos capabilities	Global mindset
(core capabilities)	Holistic decision-making

Entrepreneurial services (to deliver a WOIG-kind enterprise)	8 leadership competences
Social Contract with Business (to deliver a WOIG)	8 leadership responsibilities
Language (a new vocabulary for a WOIG)	Wisdom, love, courage
Turnaround strategy to a WOIG (to set in motion systemic success drivers of a WOIG)	18 *kairos* events
Kosoryoku (Western, Eastern and Southern values and aspirations)	Humanity's global sustainability mandate (a WOIG)
Fundamental values (what makes humanity humane?)	The Golden Rule of Humanity

Source: Author.

Knowledge clusters

Lecturing material need to incorporate the following knowledge areas:

Kairos capabilities:

> *Global mindset,* oriented towards a WOIG through:

- ◦ understanding the Social Contract with Business, that is, the letter and the spirit of the Socratic dialogue with Global Icons, humanity's global sustainability mandate, the blind spots to be eliminated, and the new language of wisdom, love, and courage;
- ◦ selected readings of an economic history of the world, globalisation, global political economy (political, economic, and legal systems), sociology, universal ethics

and values, and learning from the classics (e.g., the arts, literature, history, and anthropology);

- ◦ social, ecological, cultural, geography, and religious intelligence;
- ◦ a personal renaissance towards self-discovery;
- ◦ and mastering self-leadership.

The outcome should be a personal ethic of responsibility towards the WOIG.

➤ *Holistic decision-making*, oriented towards the turnaround to a WOIG through:

- ◦ mastering the tools of decision-making, namely, creativity; critical reasoning; systems thinking; whole brain thinking; understanding risk, uncertainty, and opportunity; intergenerational business models; management decision-making; business analysis; due diligence; complex business problem solving, and research techniques; and
- ◦ mastering the tools of buy-in of decisions, namely, communication; negotiation; influencing; crossing cultural and mindset divides; and dealing with power, ambition, and ego.

The outcome should be an ability to exercise entrepreneurial judgement.

Leadership-in-practice capabilities:

See Table 12.2 for the various knowledge clusters.

Table 12.2 The postmodern MBA's leadership-in-practice capabilities

KNOWLEDGE CLUSTERS		
Craft wealth	**Build wealth**	**Manage wealth**
Strategy	**Leadership**	**Management**
Finance	social contract with business	its processes
Marketing	entrepreneurial services	its functions
Business development	**Building the enterprise**	its skills required
international business	internal organisational design	**Functional management**
entrepreneurship	external design of global footprint	human resources
social	**Strategy implementation**	operations
entrepreneurship	project management	information
Holistic innovation	turnaround strategy	technology
management	change management	cost control
technology	**Holistic risk management**	quality assurance
business processes	corporate governance	environment
culture and mindset	enterprise—wide risk management	health and safety
	business law—local, international	
Global learning, integration, and application—the 6th sense of a WOIG business leader		

Source: Author.

Rationale: *(a) the subjects to be equally balanced between all curriculum design criteria, and should be lectured in a high-touch manner because of the high entry requirements; (b) all knowledge for the postmodern MBA's subjects is already available in the canon of business and related sciences; therefore, the professoriate only need to be tasked to compile new education material through the scholarships of discovery, integration, practice, and teaching[7]; (c) Business schools need to rediscover management as a core competence of business leadership—most firms fail because the basics are in tatters.*

In conclusion, the postmodern MBA's curriculum design is conceptualised in Table 12.3 below.

Table 12.3 The Postmodern MBA curriculum

Year or Module	Educational focus	*Kairos* capabilities		Leadership-in-practice capabilities		
		Global mindset	Holistic decision-making	Craft wealth	Build wealth	Manage wealth
1	Managing self	*	**	*	***	***
2	Managing people	*	**	*	***	***
3	Managing managers	*	**	**	***	**
4	Company manager	*	**	***	***	*
5	Managing companies	*	**	***	***	*

Note: The stars indicate the relative weight for each knowledge cluster.
Source: Author.

Implementation considerations

Although this will be country and business school specific, the overall implementation challenge would be to deal with systemic resistance to change.

Business schools are institutions that are typically incapable of fundamental change, unless being forced to do so. Since the 1950s, all fundamental changes to the MBA were as the result of external pressure. This is mainly due to its faculty having an inward looking culture, a local mindset, and an institutional culture[8] that embraces irresponsibility, self-indulgence, unaccountability, and lifelong job security. This is exacerbated by a sixty-year tradition of amoral business theory, research, case studies, and business principles[9]. Business schools have become masters at the art of illusionary transformation, and consequently need to be pulled by external events to accept change. The reasons for this strange and worrisome phenomenon are given in Appendix A.

In order to obtain a balanced view of the institutional resistance to change at business schools, it must be noted that there is a groundswell of individual academics and business school deans that are able and eager to break the glass ceiling but lack leadership and/or institutional ability and/or financial ability to deal with the risks associated with total business school transformation.

This groundswell of goodwill is the point of entry towards total business school transformation—hence, it provides for a beautiful solution.

I conclude by asking myself, 'Where will total business school transformations come from?'

In the 1950s, it was the Ford and Carnegie Foundations that intervened to radically transform American business schools after WW II.

Will history repeat itself?

I wish to acknowledge the European Foundation for Management Development who had already published parts of this chapter in the English and Chinese languages in their quarterly publication, *Global Focus*.[10,11]

I also wish to express my appreciation to the Academy of Management and Learning who commissioned a book review of my research monograph[12] which underpins this chapter.

[1]   Coetzee, J. J. 2009. A social contract with business as the basis for a postmodern MBA in a world of inclusive globalisation—A critical metasynthesis. ISBN 1-59942-290-5 (a published doctoral thesis in business leadership from the University of South Africa).

[2]   Daniel, C. A. 1998. *MBA: The First Century*. London: Associated University Press.

[3]   Benson, P. G. 2004. 'The evolution of business education in the US', *Decision Line,* January 2004.

[4]   *The Economist*, 2006. The new titans—A survey of the world economy. 16 September issue: 3-34.

[5]   Alvesson, M. and Deetz, S. 2000. *Doing Critical Management Research*. London: Sage Publications: p 146.

[6]   I have adjusted Drotter, S. J. and Charan, R. 2001. 'Building leaders at every level: a leadership pipeline', *Ivey Business Journal*, May/June: 21-27.

[7]   Boyer, E. L. 1990. 'Scholarship reconsidered', *Issues in Accounting*, 7(1): 87-91.

[8]   Stevens, G. E. 2000. 'The art of running a business school in the new millennium: a dean's perspective', *SAM Advanced Management Journal*, 65(3): 21-28.

[9]   Ghoshal, S. 2005. 'Bad management theories are destroying good management practices', *Academy of Management Learning and Education*, 4(1): 75-91.

[10]   Coetzee, J. J. 2010. The postmodern MBA—Breaking the glass ceiling. *Global Focus*, June issue.

[11]   Coetzee, J. J. 2011. The postmodern MBA—Curriculum design principles. *Global Focus*, February issue.

[12]   Book review of: A social contract with business as the basis for a postmodern MBA in a world of inclusive globalization—A critical metasynthesis. *Academy of Management and Learning*. March 2011, 10(1): 166-167.

APPENDICES

The University of South Africa is acknowledged for their kind approval to publish parts of the research methodology and its outcomes from my doctoral thesis in business leadership, titled 'Coetzee, J. J. 2009: A social contract with business the basis for a postmodern MBA—a critical metasynthesis'.

(this thesis is also available from www.dissertation.com as a research monograph, ISBN: 1-59942-290-5)

APPENDIX A

THE CONTEXT FOR CHAPTERS THREE AND TWELVE

(including a critique of the peer-reviewed academic
literature on the future of the MBA)

Introduction

In recent history, two major historical events (World War II [WW II]
and the fall of the Berlin Wall) profoundly changed the nature and
scope of the MBA (Daniel 1998, 159-180; Curtis and Lu 2004, 59).
Furthermore, it would seem that more recent events, like governance
scandals and trends towards corporate social responsibility, have
also influenced the debate on the future of the MBA. These events
and trends acted as deflection points that influenced thinking and
practice around the MBA, as expounded below.

In the contemplative years following WW II, the Ford Foundation
asked how effectively and intelligently it could put its resources
to work for human welfare. As part of an overall program to do
this, the Ford Foundation made its policy in 1950 to intervene
in business schools (B-schools) by pursuing 'The improvement
of the structure, processes, and administration of our economic
organisations: Business firms, industries, labour unions, and others'
(Carrol 1959, 155). This intervention escalated into an avalanche
of studies known as the Foundation Reports, which fundamentally
changed the philosophy, curriculum, research, and faculty of
B-schools (Benson 2004, 18-19). In this process, the MBA became

the premier qualification, in the USA and the world, for postgraduate management education, and the 'import of choice' by the countries of the developed and developing world, which needed to establish a pool of professional managers who could rebuild their economies after WW II (Friga et al. 2003, 236).

With the fall of the Berlin Wall in 1989, previously closed economies developed a seemingly insatiable demand for professional managers to convert their state-directed economies into free-market economies. This led to an unprecedented global expansion of the demand for the MBA qualification (Montgomery 2005, 150).

The governance scandals of business icons such as Enron and WorldCom caused another deflection point in the evolution of the B-schools, with an avalanche of ethics and governance courses being introduced as though business ethics never mattered before (Ghoshal 2005, 76-82).

More recent events and trends that are shaping the context wherein the debate around the MBA takes place include global socio-economic and geopolitical disturbances that could impact on the MBA's future. Examples of such disturbances and trends that are affecting the world around us include:

> the political and economic emergence of the developing countries, regarded as equally disruptive to the status quo, which was previously only matched by the Industrial Revolution—in particular, the emergence of the BRICS countries (an acronym for Brazil, Russia, India, China, and South Africa) to counter the dominant position of America and Europe ('The new titans—a survey of the world economy', *The Economist*, September 14, 2006);

> global warming, which is increasingly being accepted as a common threat to humankind's very existence on Planet Earth, thus calling for bold political, social, and business leadership (Stern Report 2007);

> the quest for intergenerational global responsibility (Global Compact; Hart 1997, 73-76);

> the discourse on the interface between business and society (Brugmann and Prahalad 2007, 82-90; April and Wilson 2007, 16-19); and

> the impact of the global economic crisis which started in 2008, and Jasmine Revolution of 2011 on the political economy of North African and Middle Eastern countries have yet to be assessed by business scientists.

Research Dilemma

As these 'events' are happening right now, it's disturbing to be reminded by Mills (1959, 3-13) that humankind is mostly incapable to understand the historical context of the time. Thus, in the debate on the future of the MBA, one would have to ask whether understanding of their own historical context is given sufficient attention by B-school academics.

Operating within such a demanding and ever-changing context, business schools (B-schools) are products of this global environment, that is, they are constructed by their contexts. However, as educational institutions and participants in shaping the context wherein they exist, they are also constructing the reality within which they operate. It therefore becomes critical to assess how B-schools reflect on the emerging world and its possible impact on themselves.

However, it's disturbing to read that the MBA 'is a 1908 degree with a 1950s strategy' (Mintzberg 2004, 7). Equally disturbing is that in the MBA curriculum design, external factors to a B-school are considered of minimal importance (Risi 2005, 75). Why are the powerful, global, socio-economic, and geopolitical forces shaping a post-WW II world order not even being considered as a factor driving MBA curriculum design, when looking at the list of ten factors driving MBA curriculum change in practice? (Risi 2005, 30). It's further disturbing to note that all fifty doctoral dissertations on the MBA over the past decade (1999-2008) focus exclusively on internal B-school efficiencies. (Proquest Dissertation and Thesis database)

Purpose and Research Objectives

This critique probes the extent to which the current discourse on the future of the MBA incorporates, or anticipates, future deflection points of a global socio-economic and geopolitical nature. The research objective is (a) to explicate the nature of the MBA discourse amongst B-school academics on the future of the MBA; and (b) to propose building blocks to align this discourse with the current discourse between global business, political and societal leaders on the nature of a post-WW II world order—the workplace of the MBA manager.

Regarding the review of the literature is critical in the sense of identifying themes, gaps, and relevance; while also being reflective in the sense of doing the critique:

> ➤ along a timeline of the evolution of the MBA since 1881—when Pennsylvania's Wharton School was established as the first business school (Daniel 1998, 29-30);

> ➤ doing the critique holistically, entering at a high level of global political, societal, and business contexts (Anshoff 1987, 501-503); and
> ➤ using only peer-reviewed research articles published in reputable academic journals have been used as the source of information, thus ignoring popular and uncontested opinions.

Such a critical and reflective critique acknowledges that the researcher's experiences and values will be reflected in the reinterpretation of known knowledge (Sandelowski 1993, 1-4). This allows the researcher to take the *bricoleur* approach of Denzin and Lincoln (1994, 4-6), where multiple research methodologies are moulded into a single research strategy to uncover the truth. In this critique current study, the author's stance is consistent with that of a researcher as *bricoleur*, since the Socratic method of systematic inquiry (Stumpf and Abel 2002, 3-4) is applied within the *kosoryoku* method of vision-making (Ohmae 2005, 271-272).

> ➤ The philosophical Socratic method uses systematic inquiry to find the truth, where the inquirer asks probing questions to which he himself does not know the answer.
> ➤ The *kosoryoku* vision-making method starts with searching for a context for the vision. In this critique, the vision making addresses two mutually exclusive questions, namely, (a) What kind of future does society desire?; and (b) What kind of society could deliver and sustain such a future?

Critique of the Discourse About the Future of the MBA

The results of the literature review reveal four distinct themes or areas of exploration by researchers, scholars, and thinkers on the future of the MBA, namely, (1) critiques of the MBA; (2) alignment of the MBA with business needs and the pursuit of knowledge creation by B-schools; (3) B-schools' strategic and operational positioning; and (4) compelling questions that are being asked.

The first theme is critique of the MBA. This theme is well published, and well summarised by Blass and Weight (2005, 230-238) in a framework they called '6 *diseases that may cause the death of the MBA*'. These six sub-themes of criticism are: (1) The patient in denial—the rhetoric and the reality gap; (2) Aspirin is the cure-all—one model fits all; (3) Waiting for the medical breakthrough—the launch of the e-MBA; (4) Misdiagnosis—reliance on league tables as a measure of quality; (5) Anorexia—every time they look in a mirror they see a 'fat MBA'; and (6) Amnesia—who or what am I? Datar, Garvin, and Cullen (2010, 8-9) continue in this tradition five years later by identifying another eight unmet needs in today's MBA, namely, (1) gaining a global perspective; (2) developing leadership skills; (3) honing integration skills; (4) recognising organisational realities and implementing effectively; (5) acting creatively and innovatively; (6) thinking critically and communicating properly; (7) understanding the role, responsibility, and purpose of business; and (8) understanding the limits of models and markets.

Whilst this type of contribution has value as a critical element of the debate, some doubts have been raised over the underlying motives for the endless list of publications under this theme. For example, it can be asked whether they are intended merely to promote personal agendas (Buono 2005, 546), to gain easy publication credits, or to make a genuine contribution to improving the MBA of the future. The counter argument to the huge body of criticism of the MBA remains largely unanswered, namely, if the MBA is that bad, why does it continue to grow in popularity the world over—isn't the customer always right, as Peters and April (2007, 19) argue? Thus, although it is indeed necessary to have such a theme, it could be that it has progressed beyond the point of diminishing returns—with too much repetition and recycling of old concerns.

Another concern is that most researchers on the MBA structure their analysis incorrectly and then reach shallow, incomplete, and misleading conclusions. The typical research design flaws are: (a) that they enter their research domain at too low a level and then mistake a part of the whole as the whole; (b) their sample of business schools are too small, and then make false truth claims; (c) to interpret a local phenomenon as a global phenomenon, and lastly (d) that personal opinions and personal opinions about other's personal opinions are mistaken as research.

The second theme is about aligning the MBA with business needs on the one hand and the pursuit of knowledge creation by B-schools on the other hand. This theme is characterised by disputes as to the relevance of business education in practice and includes constant challenges to its applicability (Starkey and Madan 2001, 3-4; Pfeffer and Fong 2002, 3-26).

It would seem that this is an ongoing bread-and-butter discourse to please various stakeholders in B-schools. However, what seems to be lacking is the challenge to seek a cooperative vision between the academic and business stakeholders. Perhaps a lesson can be learned from legal and medical schools—which also serve practice-oriented professions with academics and practitioners as stakeholders (Duncan 1971, 515-517). Thus, although this theme may be an irritation to B-school academics, it is healthy as it keeps the MBA in balance between the two worlds of business science and industry—with not too much theory and not too much skills training.

The third theme is about B-schools' strategic and operational positioning in order to remain financially viable and to grow market share. It seems that most articles in this theme provide tactical advice on organic growth and how to either catch up with competitors or leverage on industry experiences.

Whilst the first three themes are useful for the ongoing improvement and survival of B-schools and the MBA qualification, they also perpetuate the current paradigm of inward looking and repetitive thinking that largely ignores the emerging new world order. Further testimony to the inward-looking nature of the discourse on the MBA is the phenomenon that all of the 50 PhDs done on the MBA between 1999 and 2008 focused on internal B-school issues, such as improving subject, and pedagogical and delivery mode efficiencies (Proquest Dissertations and Theses: 1999-2008). Only Rissi (2005, 75) ventured slightly towards an outward-looking research theme for her doctoral study entitled 'The MBA in transition: Factors driving curriculum change'. She looked at (1) accreditation requirements; (2-4) feedback from industry, students and alumni; (5) competitive rankings; (6) program innovation and improvement; (7) globalisation of the MBA market; (8) technological advances in business; (9) internal business school resources; and (10) maintaining a competitive market share. Interestingly, yet sadly, her research concludes that factors external to B-schools play a minimal role in shaping curriculum design.

Daniel (1998: 288) concluded that the mainline MBA discourse during the twentieth century may be considered an endless cycle of the same arguments: *'The most recent comments and criticisms, as well as the most innovations by the schools, all have the same parallels in the past, often as far back as 1910 and 1915.'*

This critique reveals that Daniel's 1998 view is still valid in 2012 for the first three themes.

The fourth theme is about compelling questions that have been asked outside the other three themes. Whilst these questions are discussed directly or indirectly on a stand-alone basis, they are not articulated into the discourse on the future of the MBA. The following is a selection of the visionary questions that have been asked over the past twenty years:

➢ What is the role of management and business in society? (Drucker 1987, 18).
➢ What is the quality of academic leadership at B-schools? (Stevens 2000, 21-22).
➢ What is a business for? (Handy 2002, 54).
➢ What kind of future contextualises your vision and mission? (Ohmae 2005, 272).
➢ Why have business schools failed themselves and society? (Ghoshal 2005, 75-77).
➢ What dominant logic is required to eradicate poverty at the bottom of the human pyramid? (Prahalad 2005, 1-122).

The results of the literature review can be presented graphically in Figure A1.

Figure A1: The academic discourse about the future of the MBA

Discourse about today's MBA

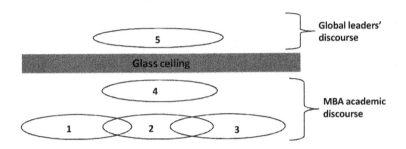

Legend: 1. Critique of the MBA
2. Closing the relevance gap – academia/business
3. Strategies to remain financially viable
4. Visionary questions, calling for change
5. Global debate on a future post WW2-world order by political, business and societal leaders

Source: Author.

The internal discourse on the future of the MBA indicated by the first three emerging themes is presented in the top half of Figure A1 (Spheres 1-3) while the fourth theme is indicated by Sphere 4.

The literature review of strategic options for graduate business schools—concepts and proposals from academics from around the world concludes:

> ➤ that, while the first three themes have received ample attention,
> ➤ the fourth theme has not yet received the same level of attention; that, while the first three themes seem mutually re-enforcing and interconnected, they are relatively unconnected to the fourth theme; and
> ➤ that the debate has until now largely ignored the emergence of a new world order. This means that the counterpoint in

the debate's internal focus, namely, focus on the global, external discourse, creates a disconnection between the MBA discourse and the global discourse, as indicated in Figure A1 as a glass ceiling. This observation is further explicated in the remaining part of this article as it provides the pointers to further discussion of the roles of B-schools.

Discussion of Building Blocks for a Postmodern MBA

The content from theme 4 points to a new global context for the future MBA, concretised in *Global Trends 2015: A dialogue about the future with nongovernmental experts* (Global Trends, 2000). This study, commissioned by the United States National Intelligence Council, provides a flexible framework for long-term strategic planning and debate. The study also provides insight into probable future deflection points of a global socio-economic and geopolitical nature, which will ultimately shape a post-WW II world order. It concludes that there are two key variables that will ultimately shape the world of tomorrow, namely, (a) the extent to which globalisation benefits the world's population, and (b) security on a global and regional scale. Depending on the ratio in which these two variables may unfold in future, four probable world orders emerge, namely, regional competition, destructive globalisation, a post-polar world, or a world order of inclusive globalisation. Each of the probable future world orders would spawn a distinctly different society, with its own values and norms, and they are graphically presented in Figure 2.1 in Chapter 2. The specific definitions for each of the four probable world orders are given at the end of the Appendix.

The current study assumes that humankind yearns for the 'Heaven on Earth' scenario, where peace or stability is the norm, and a happy and purposeful life can be lived (satisfying the universal needs of humankind of Aristotle (Stumpf and Abel 2002, 346-356). Such a state of being can only be achieved through the global pursuit of the Golden Rule of Humanity, namely, respect for, and reaching out to, one's neighbour—as advocated by all major religions of the world (Küng 1998, 97-99).

Evidence that this trend towards a world order of inclusive globalisation is already emerging is given by Prahalad (2005, 1-112) who makes a convincing case to eradicate poverty through profits. Some 70 per cent of humankind lives in a state of systemic poverty, earning less than $2 per day. He asked why we ignore the world's biggest market of some four billion people, and proposed to enter this market through a process of inclusive globalisation—the second wave of globalisation. This would require a fundamental shift in the dominant logic of business leaders, and their MBA educators. Doing just this earned the Chairperson of the Grameen Bank in Bangladesh Muhammad Yunus the Nobel Peace Prize of 2006 (see www.nobelprize.org).

Considering the scenarios referred to above and the emergence of a world order of inclusive globalisation, the debate regarding the MBA needs serious attention—which this critique shows it is not yet receiving. A discontinuity seems to exist between the internal B-school discourse and the global discourse on post WW II world order (indicated graphically in Figure A1 as the gap between 4 and 5).

This 'gap' begets a number of questions, including 'How can we unlock the current paradigm of thinking about the MBA of tomorrow, and how can we connect it with the global debate on a post-WW II world order—the future workplace of the MBA manager? What are the underlying truths pointed to by the visionary questions of the fourth theme?'

In order to find an answer to these questions, the authors reviewed literature outside the domain of traditional research, mindful of Einstein's view that the answer to a problem seldom lies on the same level as the problem. The conclusions and recommendations flowing from this critique were further enhanced by the research approach that sees the researcher as *bricoleur* (Denzin and Lincoln 1994, 4-6), and melded the Socratic method of systematically asking questions (Stumpf and Abel 2002, 3-4) with the *kosoryoku* method of vision-making (Ohmae 2005, 271-272) into a single research strategy. This led to a new set of building blocks (a new agenda) for discussing the MBA of tomorrow and unfolded (by addressing the visionary questions from the fourth theme in the context of the world order of inclusive globalisation) into a way forward, which is graphically shown in the bottom half of Figure A2.

Figure A2: A new agenda for the discourse on the future of the MBA

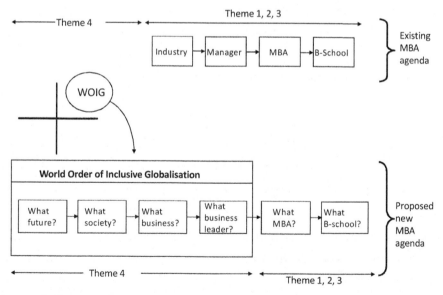

Source: Author.

The systematic questions about the new agenda for the MBA discourse that appear in the bottom half of Figure A2 can be explained as follows:

1st Socratic question: *What kind of future do we want?*

Ohmae (2005, 272) concluded his research on doing business beyond globalisation by stating that tomorrow's managers will have to apply *kosoryoku* in their strategy development—meaning that managers need to develop the ability to envision the world to come and then to shape their reality towards that vision. The author proposes that the world order of inclusive globalisation is best aligned with humankind's fundamental value system.

This poses a question about humankind's fundamental value system: Is the kind of future a business leader desires for his or her company and for his or her family the same? These two desires need to be mutually inclusive and reinforcing (unless a schizophrenic mindset guides the business leader of the future). Thus, the . . .

2nd Socratic question: *What kind of society will create this kind of future?*

Prahalad (2005, 1-112) proposed a second wave of globalisation to take the techno-economic benefits of globalisation to the bottom 70 per cent of mankind as a sustained means of eradicating poverty and countering global civil unrest. To achieve this future, it is logical to advance, not just any kind of society, but a new kind of society that aspires to a world order of inclusive globalisation.

This poses the question: What kind of society will incorporate the Golden Rule of Humanity and global stewardship as its dominant values to guide businesses? Thus, the . . .

3rd Socratic question: *What kind of business does this kind of society need?*

Handy (2002, 51-54) referred to Saint Augustine, who said that one of the greatest sins is to mistake the means for the end. Just as the sole purpose of a human being is not to eat, but to eat in order to live a purposeful life, the sole purpose of a company should be, not to make a profit, but to make a profit in order to do something meaningful. Therefore, companies should strive to become enlightened, serving all stakeholders. Handy proposed that *'We should, as charitable organisations do, measure success in terms of outcomes for others as well as for ourselves.*

This poses the question: What business leader can deliver economic prosperity as well as the values of society? Thus, the . . .

4th Socratic question: *What kind of business leader does this kind of business need?*

Drucker (1987, 13) observed (a) that there may be as much 'management' outside business as inside; (b) that modern society has become a construct of many different organisations from which members derive their livelihood, of which business is only one such societal construct; and (c) that, given the success of management, society expects more from management than that it simply generate profit. From all this, he concluded that the role of management has changed due to societal expectations, and that the consequences of this phenomenon for management theory and management practice would constitute the focus of management problems and research for the next fifty years.

This poses the question: What social contract is required between management and society in order to deliver such leadership? Thus, the . . .

5th Socratic question: *What kind of MBA does this kind of business leader need?*

Stevens (2000, 21-22) questioned the quality of academic leadership at B-schools. He asserted that top quality academic leadership is the key to coping with global, social, political, and economic trends that impact on B-schools.

In his last work before he died, Ghoshal (2005, 75-77) asked why B-schools had failed themselves and society, and called on his fellow B-school academics to reconsider the quality of their academic discourse and paradigm in order to realign them with business reality. He ascribed the necessity mainly to the constantly changing expectations of the role of organisations and managers in society.

This poses the question: Can B-schools inculcate the Golden Rule of Humanity and the social contract between management and society in the MBA curriculum? As Ole Danbolt Mjøs (Chairman of the Norwegian Nobel Committee) said upon awarding the 2003 Nobel Prize for Peace to Shirin Ebadi, 'As the university man that I am, I challenge all universities the world over to be even more distinct in underscoring the world's need for peace, democracy, and social and economic justice' (*www.nobelprize.org*). This challenge was also made by Berry (1997, 88), who asked why B-schools only promoted liberal market capitalism, and not other political philosophies like ecological conservationalism, which envisages a different future for humankind—thus, closing the loop of logic by going back to the first Socratic question (what kind of future?)!

Conclusion

Global socio-economic and geopolitical forces are shaping a new post-WW II world order. On the global stage, humankind's fate hangs in the balance while political, social, and business leaders debate the nature of such a new world order—of destructive globalisation or inclusive globalisation? The latter is of course the preferred choice of humankind, but requires a profoundly new orientation towards work and life.

For the MBA as the world's premier business qualification, a new deflection point in its evolution is required to educate business leaders to participate, contribute, and even lead in this turnaround from a world order of destruction to a world order of inclusiveness. For such a turnaround, unprecedented proportions of new business leadership competences will be required:

> through social entrepreneurship to establish a planetary middle class by eradicating systemic poverty—for this a second wave of globalisation is a prerequisite;
> through environmental entrepreneurship to surpass the Kyoto protocol requirements through technological and mindset innovations;
> through ethical entrepreneurship to marginalise the cancerous underworld economy and a consumption lifestyle, whilst establishing a global culture that embraces the Golden Rule of Humanity and global stewardship;

➢ through networking entrepreneurship to make new and unusual alliances, such as a social compact with non-governmental organisations to deliver where politicians fail society.

This critique has revealed that the current debate on the future of the MBA is too limited in scope, too inward-looking, and too isolated from the mainline global debate on the nature and dynamics of a new context for business—which is structured around perpetuating the current paradigm of the MBA. Historically, all major deflection points in the MBA's evolution have been through external shocks. B-schools are advised to anticipate a new deflection point arising from a post-WW II world order and humankind's desire for a world order of inclusive globalisation.

To reposition the MBA, brave hearts and a new agenda are called for from B-school academics. They should be mindful of the encouragement from their peers, such as Noudoushani and Nodoushani (1996, 179-180), who remind B-school faculties of their moral responsibilities to produce knowledgeable young managers who will have a profound long-term impact on their organisations and on society. B-school faculty members should be acutely aware that they engender a profound economic and socio-political impact on contemporary society.

Follow-up Research

In order to craft a new paradigm for graduate business education, the following strategic research questions come to mind, namely:

➢ What research methodology will break the MBA educational paradigm set in the 1950s by the Foundation Reports—and, has since been entrenched over nearly sixty years?

> ➢ What wisdoms and insights from global business, societal and political leaders, and thinkers, already working in or towards a world order of inclusive globalisation, may be synthesised towards a new archaeology and a new genealogy of knowledge as the basis for the transformative redefinition of a new MBA?
> ➢ What new vocabulary, new educational context, new canon of knowledge for business education, and new guidelines for curriculum design for such a postmodern MBA?
> ➢ What new research priorities for the professoriate to discover, integrate, apply, and teach such a postmodern MBA to tomorrow's business leaders?

Definitions

Kosoryoku:

A Japanese term used in strategy development. *"Kosoryoku'* is something like a "vision", but it also has the notion of "concept" and "imagination" . . . an ability to come up with a vision that is necessary and . . . implement it until it succeeds. It is . . . based on the realistic understanding of what shape the oncoming world is and, pragmatically, the areas of business that you can capture successfully because you have the means of realising the vision' (Ohmae, 2005: 271).

Golden Rule of Humanity:

As quoted by Küng (1998: 97): 'Confucius: "What you yourself do not want, do not do to another person"; Judaism: "Do not do to others what you would not want them to do to you"; Islam: "None of you is a believer as long as he does not wish his brother what he wishes for himself"; Buddhism: "A state which is not pleasant or enjoyable for me will also not be so for him; and how can I impose on another a state which is not pleasant or enjoyable for me?"; Hinduism: "One should never behave towards others in a way which is unpleasant for oneself: that is the essence of morality"; Christianity: "Whatever you want people to do to you, do also to them"'.

World order scenario 1: Inclusive globalisation (WOIG)

A virtuous cycle develops amongst technology, economic growth, demographic factors, and effective governance, which enables a majority of the world's population to benefit from globalisation. Technological developments and diffusion—in some cases triggered by severe environmental or health crisis—are utilised to grapple effectively with some problems of the developing world. Robust economic growth—spurred by a strong policy consensus on economic liberalisation—diffuses wealth widely and mitigates many demographic and resource problems. Governance is effective at both national and international levels. In many countries, the state's role shrinks, as its functions are privatised or performed by public-private partnerships, while global cooperation intensifies on many issues through a variety of international arrangements. Conflict is minimal within and amongst states benefiting from globalisation. A minority of the world's people—in sub-Saharan Africa, the Middle East, Central, and South Asia, and the Andean region—do not benefit from these positive changes, and internal conflict persists in and around those countries left behind.

World order scenario 2: Destructive globalisation (WODG)

Global elites thrive, but the majority of the world's population fails to benefit from globalisation. Population growth and resource scarcities place heavy burdens on many developing countries, and migration becomes a major source of interstate tension. Technologies not only fail to address the problems of developing countries but also are exploited by negative and illicit networks and incorporated into destabilising weapons. The global economy splits into three: growth continues in developed countries; many developing countries experience low or negative per capita growth, resulting in a growing gap with the developed world; and the illicit economy grows dramatically. Governance and political leadership are weak at both the national and international levels. Internal conflict increases, fuelled by frustrated expectations, inequities, and heightened communal tension; weapons of mass destruction proliferate and are used in at least one internal conflict.

World order scenario 3: Regional competition

Regional identities sharpen in Europe, Asia, and the Americas, driven by growing political resistance in Europe and East Asia to US global preponderance and US-driven globalisation with its own economic and political priorities. There is an uneven diffusion of technologies, reflecting differing regional concepts of intellectual property and attitudes towards biotechnology. Regional economic integration in trade and finance increases, resulting in both fairly high levels of economic growth and rising regional competition. Both the state and the institutions of regional governance thrive in major developed and emerging market countries, as governments recognise the need to resolve pressing regional problems and shift responsibilities from global to regional institutions. Given the preoccupation of all three major regions with their own concerns, countries outside these regions, in sub-Saharan Africa, the Middle East, and Central and South Asia, have few places to turn for resources or political support. Military conflict among and within the major regions does not materialise, but internal conflicts increase in and around other countries left behind.

World order scenario 4: Post-polar world

US domestic preoccupation increases as the US economy slows, then stagnates. Economic and political tension with Europe grows, the US-Europe alliance deteriorates as the United States withdraws its troops, and Europe turns inward, relying on its own regional institutions. At the same time, national governance crises create instability in Latin America, particularly Colombia, Cuba, Mexico, and Panama, forcing the United States to concentrate on that region. Indonesia also faces internal crises and risks disintegration, prompting China to provide the bulk of the ad hoc peacekeeping force. Otherwise, Asia is generally prosperous and stable, permitting the United States to focus elsewhere. Korea's normalisation and de facto unification proceed, China and Japan provide the bulk of external financial support for the Korean unification, and the United States begins withdrawing its troops from Korea and Japan. Over time, these geostrategic shifts ignite longstanding national rivalries among Asian powers, triggering increased military preparations and hitherto dormant or covert weapons of mass destruction programmes. Regional and global institutions prove irrelevant to the evoking conflict situation in Asia, as China issues an ultimatum to Japan to dismantle its nuclear programme and Japan—invoking its bilateral treaty with the United States—calls for United States reengagement in Asia under adverse circumstances at the brink of a major war. Given the priorities of Asia, the Americas, and Europe, countries outside these regions are marginalised, with virtually no sources of political or financial support.

World order scenarios: Generalisation across all 4 scenarios

The four scenarios can be grouped in two pairs: the first pair contrasting the positive and negative effects of globalisation; the second pair contrasting intensely competitive but not conflictual regionalism and the descent into regional conflict.

In all but the first scenario, globalisation does not create widespread global cooperation. Rather, in the second scenario, globalisation's negative effects promote extensive dislocation and conflict, while in the third and fourth they spur regionalism.

In all four scenarios, countries negatively affected by population growth, resource scarcity, and bad governance fail to benefit from globalisation, and are prone to internal conflict and state failure.

In all four scenarios, the effectiveness of national, regional, and international governance and the least moderate but steady economic growth are crucial.

In all four scenarios, the US global influence wanes.

(*Global Trends 2015,* 2000)

I wish to acknowledge Professor Drikus Kriek (University of the Witwatersrand) for his contributions to this essay.

APPENDIX B

GLOBAL ICON CONTRIBUTIONS

In Chapter 3, the process of selecting the Global Icons and the harvesting of their wisdom regarding the Socratic questions were introduced.

In the first part of this Appendix, the 1,000 plus wisdoms from the Global Icons are given. Thereafter the pre-selection criteria for the sample of Global Icons are introduced as well as their names.

The following is a summary of the 1,000 plus insights harvested from global leaders and the Nobel laureates, and is presented as themes of wisdom per Socratic question. Each such theme is then reclassified into one of the following turnaround strategy genres:

To be; To become: The themes of wisdom describe the end-state vision, values or nature of a WOIG.

To have; To do: The themes of wisdom describing the obstacles of a WOIG (what do I have to overcome?), the building blocks for a WOIG (what should I put in place to overcome the obstacles?), and *kairos* events (what will fundamentally move me forward to a WOIG?).

Socrates: What kind of future does humanity want?

Global leader:

Not to become   : *A future where human suffering is rife.*

To become   : *A world order, in compliance with the ideals of the United Nations.*

Nobel laureate:

Not to become   : *A growing injustice confronting humankind.*

Not to become   : *Affected by globally interconnected 'threats without borders'*

To become   : *To achieve, and maintain human security in the broadest sense*

                       : *Achievement of the United Nation's Millennium Goals*

Socrates: *What kind of society will build and sustain this kind of future?*

Global leader:

Not to become   : *A society marginalised in a globalised world*

                       : *A society ignorant of the holism of knowledge*

                       : *A society with sociological deficiencies*

                       : *A society tolerant of an abusive political system*

To become   : *A society finding its greatness in humanity, not bellicosity*

                       : *Political leaders that live up to the ideals of democracy*

                       : *A society that is protective of its rights in a democracy*

To have   : The *ability to find inclusive problem-solving approaches*

: *An entrepreneurial mindset, focussed on global stewardship*

: *The ability to make holistic strategy-making decisions*

: *The ability to plan and act in the best interest of the next generation*

: *A culture of giving*

To do   : To develop and sustain *a modern economy, driven by virtuous-cycle entrepreneurship*

: To develop a *democracy with strong checks and balances*

: To implement *improved policies timeously*

: To deliver improved services timeously *to society's basic needs*

: *To earn societal trust through measurable actions*

: *To increase global connectivity and global learning*

Nobel laureate:

Not to become   : *Society's poor understanding of social issues*

To become   : *A society with courage to 'fight the intruder' (i.e., the corrupt)*

: *A well-functioning economy*

: *A society where fundamental human rights are upheld*

: *A society whose values are deeply rooted in religious beliefs*

: *An active civil society*

To have

: *A society understanding the interconnectedness of the world*
: *An understanding of the drivers of context*
: *A realistic perception of the poor*
: The ability *to approach problems holistically*
: *Heroes and mentors of the light*
: *People making a choice for the light*
: *A love for reading and learning*

To do

: *To decommission the tools and mindsets of war*
: To communicate clearly with *all stakeholders*
: *To apply the Golden Rule of Humanity*
: *To connect like-minded people to work together*
: *To build strong democratic structures*

Socrates: *What kind of business will such kind of society require?*

Global leader:

To become

: *A world class business*
: *A business in the service of humanity*

To have

: *A strategy implementation culture*
: *The ability to understand change, and cope with it*
: *Dual leadership capabilities (i.e., local and global competence)*
: *The ability to leverage the power of knowledge*
: *The intensity to win through creativity*

To do

: *Real growth through research and innovation*
: *Real growth through collaborative strategies*
: *Real growth through strategy implementation excellence*

Nobel laureate:

To have : *Delightful organisations*

: *Respect for religious values*

To have : *Sound judgement*

: *A stable environment for sustained business*

To do : *Social entrepreneurship*

Socrates: *What kind of leader would such kind of business require?*

Global leader:

To become : *A business leader with the ability to envision the future, and to lead thereto*

: *A champion of the light*

: *A long-term wealth builder*

To have : *The ability to understand context*

: *The ability to apply intellectual thought beyond current limits*

: *The ability to make complex decisions*

To do : *To sell a vision or a purpose*

: *To cultivate an entrepreneurial culture*

Nobel laureate:

To have : *Leadership qualities of the light*

: *Intergenerational responsibility*

: *An understanding of what drives choices*

: *Empathy for the poor*

: *A love for reading and studying*

: *Courage 'to be the first drop'*

: *The ability to make complex decisions*
: *A personal renaissance*
: *Courage to apply social entrepreneurship in a big way*

To do   : *Making decisions that advance the cause of good*
: *To manage the innovation process*

For the sake of completeness, the UN's Global Compact and Millennium Goals are also tabulated below, given the Global Icon's respectful reference thereto.

Table B1: The UN's Global Compact—the ten principles

The United Nation's Global Compact is derived from the following declarations:

- The Universal Declaration of Human Rights
- The International Labour Organisation's Declaration of Fundamental Principles and Right at Work
- The Rio Declaration on Environment and Development
- The United Nation's Convention Against Corruption.

The Global Compact asks companies to embrace, support, and enact, within their sphere of influence, a set of core values in the areas of human rights, labour standards, the environment, and anti-corruption.

These ten principles are:

HUMAN RIGHTS

Businesses should

1. support and respect the protection of internationally proclaimed human rights; and
2. make sure that they are not implicated in human right abuses.

LABOUR STANDARDS

Businesses should

3. uphold the freedom of association and the effective recognition of the right to collective bargaining;
4. the elimination of all forms of forced and compulsory labour;
5. the effective abolition of child labour; and
6. the elimination of discrimination in respect of employment and occupation.

ENVIRONMENT

Businesses should

7. support a precautionary approach to environmental challenges;
8. undertake initiatives to promote greater environmental responsibility; and
9. encourage the development and diffusion of environmentally friendly technologies.

ANTI-CORRUPTION

Businesses should

10. work against corruption in all its forms, including extortion and bribery.

Source: <www.unglobalcompact.org> (Accessed on 10 September 2007)

Table B2: The United Nation's Millennium Development Goals

1. Eradicate extreme poverty and hunger.

   Target 1: Halve, between 1990 and 2015, the proportion of people whose income is less than US$1 per day.

   Target 2: Halve, between 1990 and 2015, the proportion of people suffering from hunger.

2. Achieve universal primary education.

   Target 3: Ensure that, by 2015, children everywhere, boys and girls alike, will be able to complete a full course of primary education.

3. Promote gender equality and empower women.

   Target 4: Eliminate gender disparity in primary and secondary education, preferably by 2005, and in all levels of education no later than 2015.

4. Reduce child mortality.

   Target 5: Reduce by two-thirds, between 1990 and 2015, the under-five mortality rate.

5. Improve maternal health.

   Target 6: Reduce by three-quarters, between 1990 and 2015, the maternal mortality ratio.

6. Combat HIV/AIDS, malaria, and other diseases.

   Target 7: Have halted by 2015 and begun the reverse of the spread of HIV/AIDS.

   Target 8: Have halted by 2015 and begun reverse of the incidence of malaria and other diseases.

7. Ensure environmental sustainability.

   Target 9: Integrate the principles of sustainable development into country policies and programs, and reverse the loss of environmental resources.

   Target 10: Halve by 2015, the proportion of people without sustainable access to safe drinking water and basic sanitation.

   Target 11: Have achieved, by 2015, a significant improvement in the lives of at least a hundred million slum dwellers.

8. Develop a global partnership for development.

   Target 12: Develop further an open, rule-based, predictable, and an indiscriminating trading and financial system.

   Target 13: Address the special needs of the least developed countries.

   Target 14: Address the special needs of landlocked countries and small island developing states.

   Target 15: Deal comprehensively with the debt problem of developing countries.

   Target 16: In cooperation with developing countries, develop and implement strategies for decent and productive work for young males and females.

   Target 17: In cooperation with pharmaceutical companies, provide access to affordable, essential drugs in developing countries.

   Target 18: In cooperation with the private sector, make available the benefits of new technologies and communications.

Source: <www.devdata.worldbank.org> (Accessed on 10 October 2007)

In the next section, the pre-selection criteria of the Global Icons are given.

For Global Business Leaders: (See Table B3)

Selection criteria: Two largest listed companies in each country's stock exchange. If the 2nd largest company is in the same industry sector as the largest, then the 3rd of 4th largest company was selected, but from a different industry sector. This is done to get a diversified selection of industry sectors.

Rationale: They are essentially the drivers of the Y-axis of a WOIG, with the authority and means to implement their vision.

Sources of information: Chairman's statement in the published annual report. Editorial comment and lead articles on each Chairman's global leadership from the *Financial Times* and the *Economist* in order to get a business and geopolitical perspective.

Time span: 2007.

For Global Political Leaders: (See Table B4)

Selection criteria: The current, and immediate past political leaders of each country.

Rationale: They were essentially the current drivers of the X-axis of a WOIG, with the authority and means to implement their political vision.

Sources of information: 'State of the Union' speech, or an alternative high-level speech(es) outlining their political vision.

Editorial comment and lead articles on their global leadership from the *Financial Times* and the *Economist* in order to get a business and geopolitical perspective.

Time span: 2007. For immediate past presidents, their last year in office, or a reflective speech or credible obituary during 2007.

For Global Societal Leaders: (See Table B5)

Selection criteria: The author selected societal leaders from academia. For each of the G3 and BRICS countries, a university and a business school was selected by the author, using a best fit between the following criteria: (a) the largest student-intake, (b) being recognised as influential in each country, and (c) whether the academic institution's website was available in the English language.

Rationale: They were essentially the drivers of the Y-axis of a WOIG, championing societal values, aspiration, and intellectual thought.

Sources of information: From each university's official website in English, the following was taken from each leader: His or her welcome address to the students, vision and mission statement, and one speech or publication dealing with societal values and aspirations. Editorial comment and lead articles from the *Financial Times* and the *Economist* in order to get a business and geopolitical perspective on their leadership.

Time span: 2007.

For Nobel laureates: *(See Tables B6 to B9)*

Selection criteria: The past 10 Nobel laureates for each of the peace, literature, economics and science categories: 1998-2007.

Rationale: Their work essentially drove the X-axis of a WOIG—either complementary or counter to the global political leaders. They pioneered new thinking and doing regarding world peace and stability.

Sources of information: <www.nobelprize.org>. Official press statement, the formal presentation speech by the Nobel Committee, and the formal acceptance speech of the Nobel laureate.

Given the above pre-selection criteria, the following countries, institutions, and individuals have been selected as the Global Icons:

Table B3: Global business leaders

No.	Country	Chairman and Company name	Industry sector	~Market cap. on 10 June 2007 (US$b)	Ranking
1	USA	Rex Tillerson—ExxonMobil	Energy	414	1st
2	(New York SE)	Jeffrey Immelt—General Electric	Diversified industrials	338	2nd
3	Europe (London SE)	Jorma Ollila—Royal Dutch Shell	Oil and gas	247	1st
4		Stephen Green—HSBC	Finance	224	3rd
5	Japan	Akio Mimura—Nippon Steel	Steel	16	1st
6	(Tokyo SE)	Terunoba Maeda—Mizuho Financial Group	Finance	14	2nd
7	Brazil (São Paulo SE)	José Sergio Gabrielli de Azevedo—Petrobas	Oil and gas	112	1st
8		Lazaro de Mello Brando—Bradesco	Banking	50	2nd
9	Russia(Moscow Interbank	Dmitry Medvedev—Gazprom	Natural gas extraction	225	1st
10	Currency Exchange)	Michael Prokhorov—Polyus Gold	Mining	3	4th

No.	Country	Chairman and Company name	Industry sector	~Market cap. on 10 June 2007 (US$b)	Ranking
11	India (National SE of India)	Azim Premji—Wipro Technologies	IT	13	1st
12		Harish Manwani—Hindustan Lever	Diversified retail	12	3rd
13	China (Shanghai SE)	Jiang Jianqing—Industrial and Commercial Bank of China	Finance	183	1st
14		Su Shulin—Sinopec	Petroleum	118	2nd
15	South Africa (Johannesburg SE)	Sir Mark Moody-Stuart—Anglo American	Diversified mining	91	1st
16		Meyer Kahn—SABMiller	Brewery	36	4th
			US$2,1 trillion		

Table B4: Global political leaders

No.	Country	Heads of State	Immediate past president
17-18	USA	George Bush	Bill Clinton
19-20	European Union	Jose Barroso	Romano Prodi
21-22	Japan	Yasuo Fakuda	Shinzo Abe
23-24	Brazil	Luiz da Silva	Fernando Cardozo
25-26	Russia	Vladimir Putin	Boris Yeltzin
27-28	India	Pratibha Patil	Abdul Kalam
29-30	China	Hu Jintao	Jiang Zemin
31-32	South Africa	Thabo Mbeki	Nelson Mandela

Table B5: Global societal leaders

No.	Country	Name	Position, and academic institute
33t	USA	John B. Clark	Interim Chancellor: State University of New York
34		Jay O. Light	Dean: Harvard Business School
35	Europe	Brenda Gourley	Vice-Chancellor: Open University of London
36		J. Frank Brown	Dean: INSEAD

No.	Country	Name	Position, and academic institute
37	Japan	Hiroshi Komiyama	President: Tokyo University
38		Ikeo Kyoichi	Chair of Graduate Business School: Keio University, Tokyo
39	Brazil	Suely Vilela Sampaio	Rector: University of São Paulo
40		Isak Kruglianskas	Dean: School of Business Administration FGV, University of São Paulo
41	Russia	Ludmila Verbitskaya	Rector: St Petersburg State University
42		Sergey Myasoedov	Rector: Institute of Business Studies, Academy of National Economy in Moscow
43	India	V. N. Rajasekharan	Vice-Chancellor: Indira Gandhi National Open University
44		M. K. Chaudhuri	Founder and Director of the Indian Institute of Planning and Management, New Delhi
45	China	Gu Binglin	President: Tsinghua University, Beijing
46		Yingyi Qian	Dean: School of Economics and Management, Tsinghua University
47	South Africa	Barney Pityana	Vice-Chancellor and Principal: University of South Africa
48		David Abdulai	Executive Director: University of South Africa's Graduate School of Business Leadership

Table B6: Nobel laureates for peace

No.	Date	Name	Country, date of birth	Contribution
49	2007	IPCC and Albert Arnold (Al) Gore Jr.	Geneva, Switzerland, Founded in 1988 USA, 1948	'. . . for their efforts to build up and disseminate greater knowledge about man-made climate change, and to lay the foundations for the measures that are needed to counteract such change.' [IPCC: Intergovernmental Panel on Climate Change]
50	2006	Muhammad Yunus	Bangladesh; 1940	'. . . for efforts to create economic and social development from below'

No.	Date	Name	Country, date of birth	Contribution
51	2005	Mohamed ELBaradei and IAEA	Egypt;1942 Austria; founded 1957	' . . . for their efforts to prevent nuclear energy from being used for military purposes, and to ensure that nuclear energy is used in the safest possible way' [IAEA: International Atomic Energy Agency]
52	2004	Wangari Muta Maathai	Kenya; 1940	' . . . for her contribution to sustainable development, democracy, and peace'
53	2003	Shirin Ebadi	Iran; 1947	' . . . for her efforts for democracy and human rights. She has focussed especially on the rights of women and children'
54	2002	Jimmy Carter	USA; 1924	' . . . for his decades of untiring efforts to find peaceful solutions to international conflicts, to advance democracy and human rights, and to promote economic and social development'
55	2001	Kofi Annan and the United Nations	Ghana; 1938 USA; founded 1945	' . . . for their work for a better organised and peaceful world'
56	2000	Kim Dae-jung	South Korea; 1925	' . . . for his work for democracy and human rights in South Korea and in East Asia in general, and for peace and reconciliation with North Korea in particular'
57	1999	Médicines Sans Frontièrs	Belgium; founded 1971	' . . . in recognition of the organisation's pioneering humanitarian work on several continents'
58	1998	John Hume and David Trimble	Northern Ireland; 1937 Northern Ireland; 1944	' . . . for their efforts to find a peaceful solution to the conflict in Northern Ireland'

Table B7: Nobel laureates for literature

	Date	Name	Country, date of birth	Contribution
59	2007	Doris Lessing	Persia (now Iran), 1919	'that epicist of the female experience, who with scepticism, fire, and visionary power has subjected a divided civilisation to scrutiny'
60	2006	Orhan Pamuk	Turkey; 1952	'who in the quest for the melancholic soul of his native city has discovered new symbols for the clash and interlacing of cultures'
61	2005	Harold Printer	UK; 1930	'who in his plays uncovers the precipice under everyday prattle and forces entry into oppression's closed rooms'
62	2004	Elfriede Jelinek	Austria; 1946	'for her musical flow of voices and counter-voices in novels and plays that with extraordinary linguistic zeal reveal the absurdity of society's clichés and their subjugating power'
63	2003	John M. Coetzee	South Africa; 1940	'who in innumerable guises portrays the surprising involvement of the outsider'
64	2002	Imre Kertész	Hungary; 1929	'for writing that upholds the fragile experience of the of the individual against the barbaric arbitrariness of history'
65	2001	Sir Vidiadhar Naipul	Trinidad; 1932	'for having united perceptive narrative and incorruptible scrutiny in works that compel us to see the presence of suppressed history'
66	2000	Gao Xingjian	China; 1940	'for an oeuvre of universal validity, better insights and linguistic ingenuity, which has opened new paths for Chinese novel and drama'
67	1999	Günter Grass	Germany; 1927	'whose frolicsome black fables portrays the forgotten face of history'
68	1998	José Saramago	Portugal; 1922	'who with parables sustained by imagination, compassion and irony continually enables us once again to apprehend an elusory reality'

Table B8: Nobel laureates for economics

	Date	Name	Country, date of birth	Contribution
69	2007	Leonid Hurwicz and Eric S. Maskin and Roger B. Myerson	Russia, 1917 USA, 1950 USA, 1951	'for having laid the foundations of mechanism design theory'
70	2006	Edmund Phelps	USA; 1933	'for his analysis inter-temporal tradeoffs in macroeconomic policy'
71	2005	Robert Aumann and Thomas Schelling	Germany; 1930 USA; 1921	'for having advanced our understanding of conflict and cooperation through game-theory analysis'
72	2004	Finn Kydland and Edward Presscott	USA; 1943 USA; 1940	'for their contributions to dynamic macroeconomics; the time consistency of economic policy and the drivers behind business cycles'
73	2003	Robert Engle III and Clive Granger	USA; 1942 USA; 1934	'for methods of analysing economic time series with time-varying volatility (ARCH), and common trends (cointegration) respectively.
74	2002	Daniel Kahneman Vernon Smith	Israel; 1934 USA; 1927	'for having integrated insights from psychological research into economic science, especially concerning human judgement and decision making under uncertainty' 'for having established laboratory experiments as a tool in empirical economic analysis, especially in the study of alternative market mechanisms
75	2001	George Akerlof, Michael Spence, and Joseph Stiglitz	USA; 1940 USA; during WW II USA; 1943	'for their analysis of markets with asymmetric information'

	Date	Name	Country, date of birth	Contribution
76	2000	James Heckman Daniel McFadden	USA; 1944 USA; 1937	'for their development of theory and methods for analysing selective samples, and discrete choice, respectively'
77	1999	Robert Mundell	USA; 1932	'for his analysis of monetary and fiscal policy under different exchange rate regimes and his analysis of optimum currency areas'
78	1998	Amartya Sen	India; 1933	'for his contributions to welfare economics'

Table B9: Nobel laureates for science

	Date	Name	Country, date of birth	Contribution
79	2007	Albert Fert and Peter Grünberg	France, 1938 Germany, 1938	**Physics:** ' . . . for the discovery of Giant Magneto-resistance'
80		Gerhard Ertl	Germany, 1936	**Chemistry:** ' . . . for his studies of chemical processes on solid surfaces'
81		Mario R. Capecchi, Sir Martin J. Evans, and Oliver Smithies	Italy, 1937 UK, 1941 USA, 1925	**Medicine or Physiology:** ' . . . principles for introducing specific gene modifications in mice by the use of embryonic stem cells'
82	2006	John Mather and George Smooth	USA; 1946 USA; 1945	**Physics:** ' . . . for their discovery of the black body from and anisotropy of the cosmic microwave background radiation'
83		Roger Kornberg	USA; 1947	**Chemistry:** ' . . . for his studies of the molecular basis of eukaryotic transcription'
84		Andrew Fire and Craig Mello	USA; 1959 USA; 1960	**Medicine or Physiology:** ' . . . for their discovery of DNA interference-gene slicing double-stranded DNA'

85	2005	Roy Glauber, John Hall and Theodor Hänsch	USA; 1934 Germany; 1941	**Physics:** ' . . . for their contributions to the development of laser-based precision spectroscopy, including the optical frequency comb technique'
86		Yves Chauvin and Robert Grubbs	France; 1930 USA; 1942	**Chemistry:** ' . . . for their development of the metathesis method in organic synthesis'
87		Barry Marshall and Robin Warren	Australia; 1951 Australia; 1937	**Medicine or Physiology:** ' . . . for their discovery of the bacterium *Helicobacter pylori* and its role in the gastritis and peptic ulcer disease'
88	2004	Davis Gross, David Polizer and Frank Wilczek	USA; 1941 USA; 1949 USA; 1951	**Physics:** ' . . . for the discovery of asymptotic freedom in the theory of strong interaction'

From 2008 to 2011, the wisdoms from the above Global Icons have been continuously updated to gather any new wisdoms.

APPENDIX C

SCHOLARLY CONTRIBUTIONS

(These contributions have directly or indirectly influenced my own critical thinking)

Adam, I. and Dyson, R. W. 2003. *Fifty Major Political Thinkers*. London: Routledge.

Adler, N. J. 2006. 'The arts and leadership: Now that we can do anything, what will we do?', *The Academy of Management and Learning*, 5(4): 486-499.

Adler, N. J. 2011. *Leadership Insights*. London: Routledge.

Allio, R. J. 2003. 'Russell L. Ackoff, iconoclastic management authority, advocates a systemic approach to innovation', *Strategy and Leadership*, 31(3): 19-26.

Alvesson, M. and Deetz, S. 2000. *Doing Critical Management Research*. London: Sage Publications.

Alvesson, M. and Willmott, H. 1992. *Critical Management Studies*. London: Sage Publications.

Ansoff, H. I. 1980. 'Strategic issue management', *Strategic Management Journal*, 1(2): 131-148.

Ansoff, H. I. 1987. 'The emerging paradigm of strategic behaviour', *Strategic Management Journal*, 8(6): 501-515.

April, K. and Wilson, A. 2007. 'In search of ethics: Probing the firm-society interface', *Convergence*, 8(1): 16-19.

Bair, C. R. 1999. 'Doctoral student attrition and persistence: A metasynthesis. PhD dissertation', in *Proquest Dissertations and Theses 1999*. Illinois: Loyola University of Chicago.

Bansal, P. and Corley, K. 2011. 'From the editors—The coming of age for qualitative research: Embracing the diversity of qualitative methods', *The Academy of Management*, 54 (2): 33-237.

Bateman, S. B. and Snell, S. A. 2007. *Management: The New Competitive Landscape*, 7th ed. New York: McGraw Hill.

Beck, C. 2002. 'Mothering multiples: A metasynthesis of qualitative research', *Maternal and Child Nursing*, 27(4): 214-221.

Benson, P. G. 2004. 'The evolution of business education in the US', *Decision Line*, January issue.

Berry, A. J. 1997. 'Approaching the millennium: Transforming leadership education for stewardship of the planet's resources', *Leadership and Organisation Development Journal*, 45(5): 86-92.

Blass, E. and Weight, P. 2005a. 'The MBA is dead—Part 1: God save the MBA', *Emerald Group Publishing*, 13(4): 229-240.

Blass, E. and Weight, P. 2005b. 'The MBA is dead—Part 2: Long live the MBA', *Emerald Group Publishing*, 13 (4): 241-248.

Block, P. 1993. *Stewardship*. San Francisco: Berrett-Koehler Publishers.

Boxer, L. 2011. 'Preparing leaders for a sustained future', *International Journal of Business Insights and Transformation*, 3 (special issue 3): 34-43.

Brugmann, J. and Prahalad, C. K. 2007. 'Cocreating business's new social compact', *Harvard Business Review*, February: 80-90.

Buttrick, R. 2000. *'The interactive project workout'*. London: Financial Times Prentice Hall.

Buono, A. F. 2005. 'Managers not MBAs: A hard look at the soft practice of managing and management', *Personnel Psychology*, 58(2): 543.

Campbell, R., Pound, P., Britten, N., Morgan, M. and Donovan, J. 2003. 'Evaluating meta-ethnography: A synthesis qualitative research on lay experiences of diabetes and diabetes care', *Social Science and Medicine*, 56(4): 671-684.

Carroll, T. H. 1959. 'A foundation expresses its interest in higher education for business management', *The Journal of the Academy of Management*, 2(3): 155-165.

Chomsky, N. 2006. *Failed States: The Abuse of Power and the Assault on Democracy*. New York: Metropolitan Books.

Clemmens, D. 2003. 'Adolescent motherhood: A metasynthesis of qualitative studies', *American Journal of Maternal and Child Nursing*, 28(2): 93-99.

Coetzee, J. J. 2009. A social contract with business as the basis for a postmodern MBA in a world of inclusive globalisation—a critical metasynthesis. ISBN 1-59942-290-5 (a published doctoral thesis in business leadership from the University of South Africa).

Coetzee, J. J. 2010. 'The postmodern MBA—Breaking the glass ceiling', *Global Focus*, June issue.

Coetzee, J. J. 2011. 'The postmodern MBA—Curriculum design principles', *Global Focus*, February issue.

Curtis, S. and Lu, W. 2004. 'The impact of western education on future Chinese Asian managers', *Management Research News*, 27(10): 58.

Dallmayer, F. R. 2002. 'Globalisation and inequality: A plea for global justice'. In Pasha, M. K. and Murphy, C. N. (eds.), *International Relations and the New Inequality*. Oxford: Blackwell Publishing.

Daniel, C. A. 1998. *MBA: The First Century*. London: Associated University Press.

Datar, S. M., Garvin, D. A. and Cullen, P. G. 2010. *Rethinking the MBA—Business Education at the Crossroads*. Boston: Harvard Business Press.

David, F. R. 1995. *Concepts of Strategic Management*, 5th ed. Upper Saddle River: Prentice Hall.

DeAngelo, H., DeAngelo, L. and Zimmerman, J. L. 2005. 'What's really wrong with US business schools?', <http//www.iveyemba.ca/Assets/bschoolrankings.pdf> (Accessed on 10 January 2007).

Denzin, N. K. and Lincoln, Y. S. 1994. *Handbook of Qualitative Research*. Thousand Oaks: Sage Publications.

Dixon-Krause, P. M. 2006. 'Far and creative learning transfer in management development interventions: An ecological triangulation approach to qualitative metasynthesis. PhD dissertation', In *Proquest Dissertations and Theses 2006*. Colorado: Colorado State University.

Downs, R. B. 2004. *Books that Changed the World: A Signet Classic*.

Drotter, S. J. and Charan, R. 2001. 'Building leaders at every level: A leadership pipeline', *Ivey Business Journal*, May/June: 21-27.

Drucker, P. F. 1987. 'Management: The problems of success', *Academy of Management Executive*, 1(1): 13-19.

Duncan, W. J. 1971. 'Professionalism in management and the history of administrative thought: comment', *The Academy of Management Journal*, 14(4): 515-518.

Foucault, M. 1980. *Power/Knowledge*. New York: Pantheon.

Fournier, V. and Grey, C. 2000. 'At the critical moment: Conditions and prospects for critical management studies', *Human Relations*, 53(1): 3-32.

Friga, P. N., Bettis, R. A. and Sullivan, R. S. 2003. 'Changes in graduate management education and new business school strategies for the 21st century', *Academy of Management Learning and Education*, 2(3): 233-249.

Gadamer, H. 1975. *Truth and Method*, trans. Barden, G. and Cumming, J. New York: Seabury.

Gechev, R. 2005. *Sustainable Development*. Indianapolis: Indianapolis University Press.

Ghoshal, S. 2005. 'Bad management theories are destroying good management practices', *Academy of Management Learning and Education*, 4(1): 75-91.

Giroux, H. A. and Street, P. 2003. *Shedding the Social Contract: War at Home and Abroad*. <http://www/zmag.org/content/print_article.cfm?itemID=4133andsectionID=11> (Accessed on 18 August 2006).

Global trends 2015: A dialogue about the future with non-governmental experts. 2000. USA National Intelligence Council Report.

Graham, R. J. and Englund, R. L. 2004. *Creating an Environment for Successful Projects*, 2nd ed. San Francisco: Jossey-Bass.

Grieve, K., van Deventer, V. and Mojapelo-Batka, M. 2006. *A Student's A-Z of Psychology*. Lansdowne, South Africa: Juta.

Hamel, G. 2000. *Leading the Revolution*. Boston: Harvard University Press, p. 10.

Hamel, G. 2007. *The Future of Management*. Boston: Harvard Business Press.

Handy, C. 2002. 'What's business for?', *Harvard Business Review*, 80(12): 49-55.

Hart, S. L. 1997. 'Beyond greening: Strategies for a sustainable world', *Harvard Business Review*, Jan/Feb: 67-76.

Jenson, L. A. and Allen, M. N. 1996. 'Metasynthesis of qualitative findings', *Qualitative Health Research*, 6(4): 553-560.

Kasser, T. 2002. *The High Price of Materialism*. Cambridge, MA: MIT Press.

Kedia, B. L. and Mukherji, A. 1999. Global managers: Developing a mindset for global competitiveness. *Journal of World Business*, 34(3): 230-251. Adjusted by the author.

Kennedy, H., Rosseau, A. and Low, L. 2003. 'An exploratory metasynthesis of midwifery practice in the United States', *Midwifery*, 19: 203-214.

Kerzner, H. 1998. *Project Management: A Systems Approach to Planning, Scheduling, and Controlling*, 6th ed. New York: John Wiley and Sons.

Kim, W. C. and Mauborgne, R. 2005. *Blue Ocean Strategy—How to Create Uncontested Market Space and Make the Competition Irrelevant.* Boston: Harvard Business Press.

Kothari, V. B. 2010. *Executive Greed: Examining Business Failures that Contributed to the Economic Crisis.* New York: Palgrave Macmillan.

Krefting, L. 1990. 'Rigor in qualitative research: The assessment of trustworthiness', *The American Journal of Occupational Therapy*, 45(3): 214-222.

Küng, H. 1998. *A Global Ethic for Global Politics and Economics.* Oxford: Oxford University Press.

Laszlo, E. 2006. 'Paths to a planetary civilisation', *Kosmos*, 6(2). <www.kosmosjournal.org/> (Accessed on 6 November 2006).

Lee, T. W. 1999. *Using Qualitative Methods in Organisational Research.* Thousand Oaks: Sage Publications.

Leedy, P.D. and Ormrod, J. E. 2005. *Practical Research: Planning and Design*, 8th ed., (international ed.). Upper Saddle River: Pearson Merrill Prentice Hall.

Levy, O., Beechler S., Taylor, S. and Boyaciller, N. A. 2007. 'What we talk about when we talk about 'global mindset': Managerial cognition in multinational corporations', *Journal of International Business Studies*, 38: 231-258.

Maak, T. 2009. 'The cosmopolitical corporation', *Journal of Business Ethics*, 84: 361-371.

Maak, T. and Pless, N. M. 2009. 'Business leaders as citizens of the world—Advancing humanism on a global scale', *Journal of Business Ethics*, 88: 537-550.

Mills, C. W. 1959. *The Sociological Imagination*. London: Oxford University Press.

Mintzberg, H. 2004. *Managers Not MBA's: A Hard Look at the Soft Practice of Management and Management Development*. San Francisco: Berrett-Koehler Publishers.

Mintzberg, H. and Westley, F. 2001. 'Decision-making: It's not what you think', *MIT Sloan Management Review*, 42(3): 89-93.

Moldoveaunu, M. C. and Martin, R. L. 2008. *The Future of the MBA—Designing the Thinker of the Future*. New York: Oxford University Press.

Montgomery, D. B. 2005. 'Asian management education: Some twenty-first century issues', *Journal of Public Policy and Marketing*, 24(1): 150-154.

Morleau, G. L. 2004. *The Ultimate MBA—Meaningful Biblical Analogies for Business*. Minneapolis: Augsburg Books.

Mouton, J. 2005. *How to Succeed in Your Master's and Doctoral Studies: A South African Guide and Resource Book*. Pretoria, SA: Van Schaik.

Nain, M. 2006. *Illicit: How Smugglers, Traffickers, and Copycats are Hijacking the Global Economy*. Privately published through Eric Olsen Publishers, USA.

Noblit, G. W. and Hare, R. D. 1988. *Meta-Ethnography: Synthesizing Qualitative Studies*. Newbury Park, CA: Sage Publications.

Nodoushani, O. and Nodoushani, P. 1996. 'Rethinking the future of management education', *Human Systems Management*, 15(3): 173-181.

Ohmae, K. 2005. *The Next Global Stage: Challenges and Opportunities in Our Borderless World*. Upper Saddle River: Wharton School Publishing.

Palmer, J. A. (ed.). 2001. *Fifty Key Thinkers on the Environment*. London: Routledge.

Parnel, J. A. and Dent, E. B. 2009. 'Philosophy, ethics and capitalism: An interview with BB&T Chairman John Allison', *Academy of Management Education and Learning*, 8(4): 587-596.

Paterson, B., Thorne, S. and Dewis, M. 1998. 'Adapting to and managing diabetes', *Image Journal of Nursing Scholarship*, 30(1): 57-62.

Penrose, E. T. 1959. *The Theory of the Growth of the Firm*. Oxford: Basil Blackwell.

Peters, K. and April, K. 2007. 'The global future of the MBA', *Convergence*, 7(4): 16-19.

Pfeffer, J. and Fong, C. T. 2002. 'The end of business schools? Less success than meets the eye', *Academy of Management Learning and Education*, 1(1): 78-95.

Pielstick, C. D. 1998. 'The transforming leader: A meta-ethnographic analysis', *Community College Review*, 26(3): 15-33.

Porter, M., Lorsch, J. W. and Nohria, N. 2004. 'Seven surprises for new CEOs', *Harvard Business Review*, 82(10): 62-72.

Prahalad, C. K. 2005. *The Fortune at the Bottom of the Pyramid: Eradicating Poverty Through Profits*. Upper Saddle River: Wharton School Publishing.

Pressman, S. (ed.) 1999. *Fifty Major Economists*. London: Routledge.

Quilligan, J. B. 2008. 'Making the great adjustment: Coalition for the Global Commons', *Kosmos*, Summer: 67-69.

Risi, K. M. 2005. The MBA in transition: Factors driving curriculum change. Doctoral thesis. Publication number AAT 3182866. Pennsylvania: Drexel University.

Roglio De Déa, K. and Light, G. 2009. 'Executive MBA programs: The development of the reflective executive', *Academy of Management learning and Education*, 8(2): 256-173.

Ryan, M. J. and Barclay, D. W. 1987. 'Integrating results from independent studies', *Advances in Consumer Research*, 10(1): 492-496.

Samuel, S. 1996. 'Mary Parker-Follet—Prophet of management: A celebration of writings from the 1920s [Book Review]', *Academy of Management Journal*, 21: 863-867.

Sandelowski, M. 1993. 'Rigor or rigor mortis: The problem of rigor in qualitative research', *Advances in Nursing Sciences*, 8(3): 1-8.

Sandelowski, M., Docherty, S. and Emden, C. 1997. 'Qualitative metasynthesis: Issues and techniques', *Research in Nursing and Health*, 20: 365-371.

Sernak, K. S. 2008. 'School reform and Freire's methodology of conscientization', In Anthony H. Normore (ed.), *Leadership for Social Justice: Promoting Equity and Excellence Through Inquiry and Reflective Practice*. Charlotte, NC: Information Age Publishing, pp. 115-149.

Sherwood, G. 1997a. 'Metasynthesis: Merging qualitative studies to develop nursing knowledge', *International Journal for Human Caring*, 3(1): 37-42.

Sherwood, G. 1997b. 'Metasynthesis of qualitative analysis of caring: Defining a therapeutic model of nursing', *Advanced Practice of Nursing Quarterly*, 3(1): 32-36.

Silverman, D. 1997. 'Towards an aesthetics of research', In Silverman, D. (ed.), *Qualitative Research Theory, Method, and Practice*. London: Sage Publications, pp. 239-253.

Simpson, D. (ed.) 2006. *Fifty Key Thinkers on Development*. London: Routledge.

Sipe, T. A. 1995. A metasynthesis of educational achievement: A methodological approach to summarisation and synthesis of meta-analysis. PhD dissertation. Georgia: Georgia State

University. In *Proquest Dissertations and Theses 1995*. Section 0079, Part 0288, Publication Number AAT 9610052, 304 pages.

Starkey, K. and Madan, P. 2001. 'Bridging the relevance gap: Aligning stakeholders in the future of management research', *British Journal of Management*, 12(Special Issue): S3-S26.

Starkey, K. and Tempest, S. 2009. 'The winter of our discontent: The design and challenge for business schools', *Academy of Management Learning and Education*, 8(4): 576-586.

Starkey, K. and Tiratsoo, N. 2007. *The Business School and the Bottom Line*. Cambridge: Cambridge University Press.

Stern, P. and Harris, C. 1985. 'Women's health and the self-care paradox: A model to guide self-care readiness—Clash between the client and the nurse', *Health Care for Women International*, 6: 151-163.

Stevens, G. E. 2000. 'The art of running a business school in the new millennium: A dean's perspective', *SAM Advanced Management Journal*, 65(3): 21-28.

Stumpf, E. S. and Abel, D. C. 2002. *Elements of Philosophy: An Introduction*, 4th ed. New York: McGraw-Hill.

The Economist. 2006. 'The new titans: A survey of the world economy', *The Economist*, 16 September: 3-34.

Thompson, A. A. and Strickland, A. J. 1998. *Strategic Management: Concepts and Cases*, 10th ed. New York: McGraw-Hill.

Walsh, D. and Downe, S. 2005. 'Metasynthesis method for qualitative research: A literature review', *Journal of Advanced Nursing*, 50(2): 204-211.

Werther Jr., B. and Chandler, D. 2010. *Strategic Corporate Social Responsibility: Stakeholders in a Global Environment*. Thousand Oaks: Sage Publications.

Wogaman, J. P. 1977. *Christians and the Great Economic Debate*. London: SCM Press.

Yardley, L. 2000. 'Dilemmas in qualitative health research', *Psychology and Health*, 15: 251-228.

Yunus, M. 2007. *Creating a World Without Poverty*. New York: Public Affairs.

Acknowledgement: dreamstime.com for the world map on the cover page

CPSIA information can be obtained at www.ICGtesting.com
Printed in the USA
BVOW08s2203050815

412066BV00001B/30/P